"*Beyond Belief* is an invitation to rethink hov build confidence in ourselves and others. N trusting and authentic relationships that en experience more than they ever thought p(us to coach from the heart and soul – emb the journey, and staying true to ourselves. If you're curious about the art of fostering a deep experience of confidence, belonging, and growth in those you support, this is a must-read."

Katie Mobed – performance psychologist at The Prime Clinic and co-author of *You Are a Champion* with Marcus Rashford

Mike Porteous gives me confidence – pun intended – that coaching is on the right path. *Beyond Belief* transcends the regular predictable coaching book. In fact, I would call it more of spiritual guide, with deep insights the likes of which I've never seen before. A must-read for any coach who is pursuing mastery of their craft."

Cody Royle – coach to head coaches in elite sports and author of *Second Set of Eyes*, *The Tough Stuff* and *Where Others Won't*.

"*Beyond Belief* is a transformative book that is a must read for anybody serious about helping people reach their potential. Mike Porteous masterfully weaves together research, personal insights and real-life experiences to introduce the concept of 'confidence-centred coaching', an approach that reshapes not only how we support athletes but also how we understand personal growth and human connection.

"This book is not just for coaches but for anyone seeking to inspire and empower others. It offers a compelling argument for putting confidence at the heart of all we do, challenging conventional wisdom and inviting readers to embrace creativity, empathy and self-awareness. His insights into the art of coaching, enriched by reflective conversations with experts and practitioners, open up a uniquely humane vision of what coaching can achieve.

"*Beyond Belief* provides a roadmap for creating meaningful, transformative relationships rooted in trust, authenticity and purpose. This is a must-read for anyone who believes in the power of confidence to unlock human potential."

Stuart Armstrong – Head of Coaching at Sport England and host of the Talent Equation podcast

"*Beyond Belief* by Mike Porteous is a transformative read for anyone guiding others in life or sport. Rather than a traditional coaching manual, it is a profound exploration of confidence, trust, and meaningful connection at the heart of true coaching. Mike's insights offer a fresh perspective, challenging us to rethink success and nurture environments where individuals surpass their expectations. This book is essential for leaders ready to inspire authentic growth and resilience through the quiet power of belief."

Jen Coe – Performance Well-being Lead, The FA (Women's Professional Game) and co-editor of *Myths of Sport Coaching* and *Myths of Sport Performance*

"*Beyond Belief* challenges us to reconsider how we build the confidence of those in our care. Cherishing individuality, committing deeply to the relationship between person and environment, and favouring, not the accumulation of knowledge for dissemination, but the embrace of not knowing and of a journey orientation. If you are curious to learn more about developing a deep sense of identity, belonging, and confidence in those you are fortunate to support, then I highly recommend giving this book your time."

Craig Morris – Olympic canoe slalom coach and high performance coach consultant

"Mike has taken coaching, re-imagined it, and put confidence at the heart, helping coaches understand how to nurture it. With numerous remarkable stories for you to think with and bucket loads of practical examples, it's a must read for anyone who thinks confidence is helpful!"

Rusty Earnshaw – Director of The Magic Academy and international performance rugby coach

"The philosophy we work from at The True Athlete Project is one of a more compassionate, mindful approach to sport. Mike's approach to coaching positively hums with resonance with this approach, and so it was a great pleasure to see this shine through in such a practical format as is presented here. The fact that Mike frames coaching among words such as artistry, kindness, beauty, and magic gives you a sense that this is not a standard coach development text. Far more than that, it is a philosophy in itself, and one that is wonderfully aligned with embracing the human that is doing the coaching, promoting their flourishing alongside the people they are in a coaching relationship with.

"This is precisely the shift of coaching practice that I would love to see more fully embraced in the world, at all levels of sport. If that were to happen, I have no doubt that we would see a whole host of more positive outcomes, not least in even better performances!"

Laurence Halsted – The True Athlete Project

"Loved it!! Sometimes reading about a different discipline is an open invitation to think differently and make meaning in our own craft. Mike's optimistic and clear approach holds some golden nuggets of wisdom for any coach of anyone."

Claire Pedrick MCC – winner of the Outstanding Contribution to Coaching Award 2022 from Henley Business School and co-author of *The Human Behind the Coach*, winner of Specialist Business Book 2024

"It sings!"

Professor Stephen Rollnick – co-founder of Motivational Interviewing and co-author of *Coaching Athletes to Be Their Best*

BEYOND BELIEF

The art of confidence-centred coaching

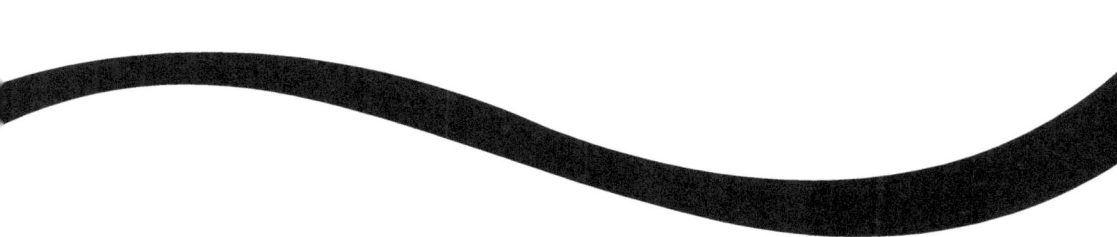

MIKE PORTEOUS

First published in Great Britain by Practical Inspiration Publishing, 2025

© Mike Porteous, 2025

The moral rights of the author have been asserted

ISBN   978-1-78860-716-2   (hardback)
            978-1-78860-717-9   (paperback)
            978-1-78860-719-3   (epub)
            978-1-78860-718-6   (Kindle)

Every effort has been made to trace copyright holders and to obtain their permission for the use of copyright material. The publisher apologizes for any errors or omissions and would be grateful if notified of any corrections that should be incorporated in future reprints or editions of this book.

Part page illustrations by Cave & Sky @caveandsky.
Back cover photo by Sam Shaw.
Author photo by Vivienne Rickman.

Want to bulk-buy copies of this book for your team and colleagues? We can customize the content and co-brand *Beyond Belief* to suit your business's needs.

Please email info@practicalinspiration.com for more details.

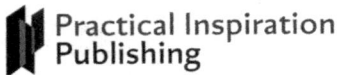

Practical Inspiration Publishing

This book is lovingly dedicated to some wonderful women: Anne, Mariê, Jenni and Chloe;

to the equally wonderful Thomas and Miles;

and in memory of Marta.

Table of contents

"What wisdom can you find that is greater than kindness?"

Jean-Jacques Rousseau

Foreword

THIS BOOK IS an extraordinary and beautiful read, not only for sports coaches, but also for any parent, teacher or leader. It's a book for our times with much-needed insights for our sports clubs and schools, homes and workplaces. Confidence is a concept that is much talked about but often poorly understood and therefore even more poorly taught and developed. *Beyond Belief* offers an important reframe and reset, based on both research and Mike's powerful stories and real-life experiences. This book will bring you ideas and inspiration as a sports coach that will work in any walk of life.

We are in a time where we need sport and physical activity, and the inherent ability to explore our potential, to play a different and much more central role in our lives. Our society needs us to become a healthier nation of connected communities, with less inequality and burnout and greater opportunities for our young people, with a real resilience to navigate the fast-paced, changing world we live in. Mike's insights and pathway to building a more profound type of confidence offer a crucial step toward creating healthier experiences in sport, and through that, understand routes to leading healthier, happier lives.

This new theory and practice of confidence shows that the path to becoming a better coach of confidence in others is also a path to better understanding ourselves. This book goes way beyond any practical how-to manual – we have no need for that – to offer a beautiful and, at times, magical read. It both challenges and supports us to reconsider our beliefs and patterns of thinking, our habits and behaviours, our creativity and self-awareness, and our daily interactions and impact on others.

I have loved reading and seeing this book develop. As someone who has spent a lifetime in sport, from growing up with the label of "non-sporty" at school and losing all self-confidence, to finding and falling in love with the sport of rowing at university, and then going on an unexpected journey to becoming a triple Olympian, I wish that I had come across a coach like Mike. But I hope that through this book, Mike's insights and approach will reach many more coaches and people wanting to discover the self-confidence to explore what they're capable of. For some in sport that might be overcoming a fear of water or trying to become an Ironman. For others, it could be any aspect of life where we want to explore our potential a little further or discover if we can take the next step toward our ambitions. This is a journey we all need to go on.

Dr Cath Bishop
Olympian, former diplomat, culture coach, author of *The Long Win*

Preface

How do you think of confidence? And what part does it play in how you support others to great endeavours in sports? I want to introduce you to a way of coaching, with confidence at its heart, that can have the most wonder-filled, extraordinary effects – for the coach and those we coach.

The starting point is that confidence and self-belief, though much referred to, have yet to be fully grasped and made the centre of what I believe can be extraordinary coaching practice – across all sports and for coaching all ages, abilities and ambitions. It requires some courage to rethink many of the approaches and assumptions we make about the way a coach should be and act, how we view great coaching, what we aspire to and where we look for models to learn from.

At the same time there is something fundamental and far-reaching underway in our sports world – one that I believe the ideas and practices of a confidence-centred coaching belong to and can contribute to in a powerful, creative way. A shift is emerging, though seen in glimpses and forms that have yet to fully take shape. You see it in the growing focus in some coaching forums on self-awareness and reflection, so-called "holistic" and "athlete-centred" coaching, co-creation, wholeness and wellbeing and more. It's there in the occasional stories of a few standout coaches forging very different ways of working, who talk of caring and personal growth – though still as all too rare glimpses of alternatives to the mainstream, conventional ways of coaching that still hold sway. I believe that if we rethink what we understand by confidence and the part it can play in all that we do, we open up a much wider view of how different being a coach could be, the places we coach in and the impacts we have.

Fundamentally the book is coming from a place of yearning for a better way of supporting those we are privileged to be with. One that is rooted in care and kindness, to ourselves as well as others. That revels in an artistry and magic of coaching far beyond conventional instructional prowess. That seeks to develop deep, meaning-filled relationships of trust, and looks to create cultures in our sports organizations and clubs that serve a higher purpose than winning medals or trophies (though they will surely follow). So we start with looking at confidence and move into a wider, even richer changing landscape.

You probably realize this book is unlike any coaching book you will have come across: not a "how to" manual, though full of practical insights; more an invitation to rethink and re-imagine how much better our coaching could be. For us and those we coach. And in its focus on confidence there are no one size fits all prescriptions of what to do or say. Instead, an emphasis on truly knowing in ourselves, often before the words, what is felt. In essence the approach is all about the coach and coached finding an easy fluency, being wholly attuned – mind and body – to self and others and a depth of meaningful connections. A key measure of success will be us and those we coach surprising ourselves with what we can do. Beyond belief coaching.

Another unconventional feature that I hope will come through is beauty. Beauty as in those magical, surprising moments when we find ourselves captured by what we see or hear; aware it somehow affects us yet unsure how or why. Time briefly stands still. There's a calming, possibly humbling moment of quietness as we take in what is before us; maybe feel a deep connection, touching something inside us – all in the realm of feeling and sensations without words. We will see these themes running through the book: connections to deeper feelings, a sense of wonder in the stillness and an openness to the magic of the moment.

Now, however you may think of it, beauty is not a notion you would typically associate with coaching. It certainly doesn't appear in the textbook-type prescriptions of how to coach, nor in any courses I have come across. Yet there is a profound and magical beauty in the skilful craft, creative artistry and deep connections our approach is anchored in and the possibilities it opens up. And the results can have a powerful, moving beauty way beyond how we normally measure sporting success.

So the book is as much an introduction to confidence at the heart of great coaching as an invitation to re-imagine a coaching landscape that has a profound beauty, marked by kindness and boldness in its practices and ambitions.

Warriors, pioneers and leaders

Before we set off, a few words on where the ideas and practices come from.

Whilst there are well grounded theoretical and evidence-based foundations for many of the ideas and practices outlined in this book[1], the biggest single debt of gratitude is to the wonderful women, men and young people who I have been lucky enough to coach over many years. So we start with them.

There is something alluring that seems to draw different people to endurance activities – and in that way, a few to me for coaching. Some of those I've worked with include women who learnt to swim as children (after a fashion) but for the rest of their lives kept well away from anything resembling what they typically call "proper swimming" and now want to get into open water swimming. Above all, they want to feel good at something and maybe complete a daunting event like a 5k or 10k river swim. Or (as I know from my experience) relatively seasoned sprint or standard distance triathletes taking on longer and more arduous challenges, "moving up" as they would say to a half or full Ironman distance. Then taking on yet more extreme challenges, as if completing a 9–16 hour event wasn't enough. Others include marathon runners chasing personal best times that they somehow feel are still in them but remain out of reach. I have been enormously privileged to work with and support many such aspiring individuals, each with their own story and personal challenges to reach beyond what they thought was possible. They provide the breath and life for the book.

We will come across some of their stories and lessons:

- a young, teenage woman, brimming over with so much motivation and energy that you wonder if it could be somehow bottled and shared around

- a distance runner preparing his mental strategies, along with his sparse kit and nutrition, for the six-day epic Marathon des Sables through the Sahara Desert

- a super-talented, yet unknown runner showing up for her first track session in a new town, a new club

---

[1] For those after more academic, well-referenced guides, try A. Whitehead and J. Coe (eds) *Myths of Sport Coaching* (2021), or C. Nash (ed) *Developing Sports Coaches* (2023).

- a GB athlete battling with undermining fears of coming off their super-light, precarious time trial bike at speed… and many more.

And here's the thing. We often think of the best coaching as being at the higher, elite or professional levels – and for sure there are some impressive big names to learn from. However, these assumptions and preconceptions about the best of coaching belong to a different, I believe limiting and outdated landscape that we want to move away from. Some of the most skilful, impactful coaching takes place out of the limelight, through what my mentor Stephen Rollnick would call a "calm, compassionate, curious" attentiveness to the person in front of us – and without a relentless focus on achieving narrowly defined end results. And our greatest teachers are the very people we aim to coach as they wrestle with a yearning desire to accomplish whatever may be their challenge, often whilst plagued by self-doubt or fear of failure. Such resolute warriors[2] make this book possible – with enormous gratitude for their openness and trust.

A second invaluable source drawn on in this book is interviews and research into the work of other coaches from across a wide range of sports. As will be seen, there is also a strong emphasis on looking at leaders in other fields beyond sports who have great insights to offer. A few of these are captured at the end of each chapter in what are called Reflective Conversations – accounts of in-depth interviews and discussions I had in researching and exploring ideas for the book that help bring new perspectives and insights to each chapter.

Many exchanges with other coaches in various forums across sports have also helped develop the ideas in this book – bringing new perspectives and challenging views. These include workshops and informal sessions through a network I set up for coaches with a shared interest in confidence. I also belong to several other networks that meet regularly – a self-support peer group of triathlon coaches, others for coaches and coach developers across all sports and a local group of psychologists. Mentoring other coaches and being mentored has also added to the deep well of shared ideas and experiences. And it is the openness to talk through and share our experiences and challenges that I really value. I think this brings a sense of being pioneers – of setting out to look for and discover new ways of doing things, of feeling our way, learning from each other and being honest about our doubts, rather than acting as if we know it all.

---

[2] The phrase comes from The School of Life *Art Against Despair* (2022).

We will also see in the book a quest to find leaders in other fields. If we want to develop our skills in, for example, empathetic listening, for sure we may find some great examples amongst our coaching colleagues – yet we can also look for leaders in unrelated fields where these skills have to be at their sharpest and most developed. The cutting edge of empathy. One of our Reflective Conversations is with a psychotherapist who specializes in work with young people experiencing harmful addictions: listening, empathy and trust far out at a frontier way beyond what we typically face in our coaching.

Similarly with creativity. I know some gifted coaches who come up with highly imaginative, playful sessions and encourage me to be braver, take risks and try the untried. At the same time, I believe we can also learn from certain artists – painters, dramatists, musicians, dancers and choreographers – any whose expressive work takes us to new, unimagined places. Of special interest, we can learn from those who engage and draw in others with little or no background in the arts to create highly innovative, moving and enriching collaborative work. We'll meet some unlikely young stars along the way, as well as one such artist, a choreographer of deeply impactful participative work, in another of the Reflective Conversations.

So, a rich mix of leading pioneers and pioneering leaders.

Throughout the book we will draw on and, in places, stop to take in the work of a wide range of researchers, psychologists and many other experts whose bold ideas have shaped the thinking – some relatively well known in sports coaching, others from very different backgrounds and interests[3]. I feel an enormous sense of gratitude to all.

Structure of the book

A few words to guide us through the book. If it's not too clichéd, think of it as a journey of discovery.

Part 1 maps out where we are and what confidence looks and – most important – feels like. Chapter 1 introduces some imagery and a framework that we can refer to as we embark on discovering how to put confidence at the centre of all we do. With the help of some leading lights we'll introduce some key principles to guide us along the way.

---

[3] References will be footnoted for those who want to follow up sources.

Chapter 2 dives in to rethinking confidence. This sets out a key theme of focusing on what is *felt* in order to arrive at a deeper understanding of confidence and self-belief – for coaches and those we coach.

Part 2 then takes us into three domains of confidence and is the heart of the book:

- Chapter 3: Confident coaches explores how we can develop and nurture our own confidence and create coaching spaces in which we feel assured and let the coaching flow

- Chapter 4: Confidence in the coach opens up the development of trusting relationships, rooted in meaningful connections. This chapter also looks at when things go wrong

- Chapter 5: Coaching for confidence turns to how we can support and encourage the confidence of those we coach as they face their challenges. This introduces a model I have developed and use with clients: the Four Ps of Confidence-Centred Coaching.

Part 3 then uses the prism of confidence to open up and look at key areas of coaching in our changed landscape, revealing how much of our thinking, practices and received wisdom is changed by putting confidence at the heart of all we do. Chapters 6–9 explore:

- The magic of creativity as a fundamental, defining characteristic of coaching all ages and abilities

- Motivation and the paradoxes of inner drives, revealing contradictory emotions and looking at what gets in the way

- Resilience at the outer edges, drawing on lessons from adversity and being in a place of pain

- Protecting our coaching energy completes our journey by addressing the threat of burnout and exhaustion. This explores the qualities of coaching energy to be sought out and nurtured, with a big emphasis on caring for ourselves as we face continuing challenges.

We end with a short final look at the wider, richer landscape of coaching that our journey has opened up to us.

Let's begin.

Part 1
Setting off to discover confidence

1
Where we are

"What if…?"

Opening question for confidence-centred coaching workshops

IN THIS BOOK we are going to fundamentally rethink how we understand confidence and its place in all we do – and in that way we will challenge many of the most basic assumptions we make about great coaching. So a map of where we are and aim to get to and some navigational aids to guide us on our way will help at the outset.

In this chapter we will:

- introduce an image that helps orientate ourselves as we look to shift from one world view to another

- see how different central, focal points lead to very different ways of operating as coaches, what we aspire to and how we deepen our practice

- identify some guiding principles to help illuminate the way forward

- see how our first Reflective Conversation illustrates something of this uneasy navigation whilst also giving an insightful example of how rich and powerful our coaching can be when we can make a shift.

Fish and birds

Moving from one way of being, from looking at the world in one way and switching to another, is far from easy. The shape of the new way of doing things is rarely clearly visible and so much of our thinking, the assumptions we make about what counts as good coaching and how we are judged (and judge ourselves) belong to the very world we are trying to move away from. How to make sense of a new landscape and way of being?

M.C. Escher's 'Sky and Water I*' © 2024 The M.C. Escher Company – The Netherlands – All rights reserved. www.mcescher.com*

A particular image comes to mind that will help us locate where we are. Have a look at this captivating etching by Dutch artist M.C. Escher. His designs of transitions from one world to another offer an intriguing, insightful way of thinking about the in between states as we shift from what some might call one paradigm – our notions of the world, what works and how things should be – to a new one.

Under the water, we see clearly defined, easily recognizable fish. Moving upwards, the fish begin to lose their compelling detail and somehow the shape of something different starts to emerge, indistinct and unconnected at first. We begin to see the outline of a transition, but it remains unclear, hard to make out and somehow fragmented. Only finally do we see clearly distinct, fully formed birds flying high in the clear sky.

In much the same way, it is as if we are straining to make out the shape of a new paradigm or landscape of coaching but are still caught in that murky middle – ready to leave the old, familiar ways behind but not quite able to make out the fully formed shape and detail of how different it could be. Many of the questions we ask of ourselves, and others put to us, the expectations and assumptions about great coaching, how we are judged and how we judge ourselves belong below the surface to a deeply ingrained, traditional world of coaching – the coach as the expert, the arbiter of what is right, and those we coach as more or less compliant recipients of our expert knowledge and experience.

Here's a question that may illustrate the point: how do you get and hold the attention of those you coach? Is it the conventional, taken for granted way that simply by occupying the role of coach we should expect some degree of attentiveness and respect from those in front of us, COACH printed on our top as a stamp of authority? Is it by the accumulation of qualifications and so many years of experience that supposedly denotes a command of fine technical knowledge and expertise that we stand ready to impart? A hard-earned reputation for previous successes with high-performing athletes or teams? Think of the way we were taught to act as coaches, the what to do of coaching: to plan-do-review, to project, command the space and keep order. All very sound and deserving of respect for sure – but what would holding attention, generating engagement and shared energy look like if we put confidence at the very centre of our coaching?

As we will see in the book, there are three key dimensions or domains of confidence in which this might take shape:

- *our own confidence and self-belief as a coach* will lie in grounding ourselves in what is unique to each of us, an awareness and acceptance of who we truly are and a clear sense of our values

- *the confidence those we coach have in us* will come from the quality of connections and trust we develop with each individual, rather than a position of authority or even past success with others (commendable and valuable though these are)

- *and how we support their confidence and self-belief to face their challenges* will be rooted in them truly knowing and feeling in themselves the extraordinary power and potential of what they can do, rather than any expert knowledge or special gifts we have.

Each of these will be explored more fully in the book – not just to answer the question of how we gain others' attention but more widely: what it means to be confident coaches, creating assured spaces for ourselves and others; how we develop relationships of trust in which those we coach come to have confidence in us; and how we can coach in such a way as to help nurture their own confidence and self-belief. Confident coaches, confidence in the coach and coaching for confidence. But we are jumping ahead of ourselves!

Coaching circles

Like much of the book, let's turn to a personal story.

When I was qualifying as a triathlon coach, going through successive levels and awards, the higher one went, the stronger the focus on *performance*. How to analyse a triathlete's strengths and weaknesses, how to design rigorous training programmes to peak at just the right time or work on improving technical aspects of their swimming, cycling or running. We were fortunate to have inputs from some of the UK's top experts in specialisms such as programme design, physiology, psychology, swim technique, nutrition and much more. With this expert knowledge we would be equipped to coach athletes at the highest, competitive levels. Yet there seemed to me to be at least two things missing.

One was that several of the coaches on the highest level programme were involved in club coaching for young athletes and relative newcomers, rather than elites. For them (and me as my interests straddled both) it seemed a *developmental* focus was far more relevant: how to impart skills and a joy for our sport. As we will see, very different criteria come into play.

The other missing focus seemed to me to come to light each evening after class when we sat around, chatting about what we had learnt, how we might apply it in our different club settings or with those we coach. A repeated theme was all about *confidence*. Would I feel ready to try out some of the techniques and methods on my clients and in the club where I was Head Coach? We also often talked about the difficult relationships we had with some of those we coached. Most common of all in our conversations was the all-important confidence factor in those we coached: how to help the unmotivated or those who come full of self-doubt. Several of us shared similar stories of athletes with great potential who somehow never realized it in the heat of competitions, despite our very best efforts at expert preparation.

This led me to identify three distinctive, though overlapping focal points for coaching.

Coaching circles

Performance-centred:
- narrow focus on results: podium places, times, the finish line/final whistle
- objective measures and evidence-based methods
- deepen expertise by technical/ tactical knowledge

Development-centred:
- open focus on skills and love for the sport
- looser measures of engagement (e.g. retention)
- deepen expertise by making learning fun and enjoyable (e.g. FUNdamentals)

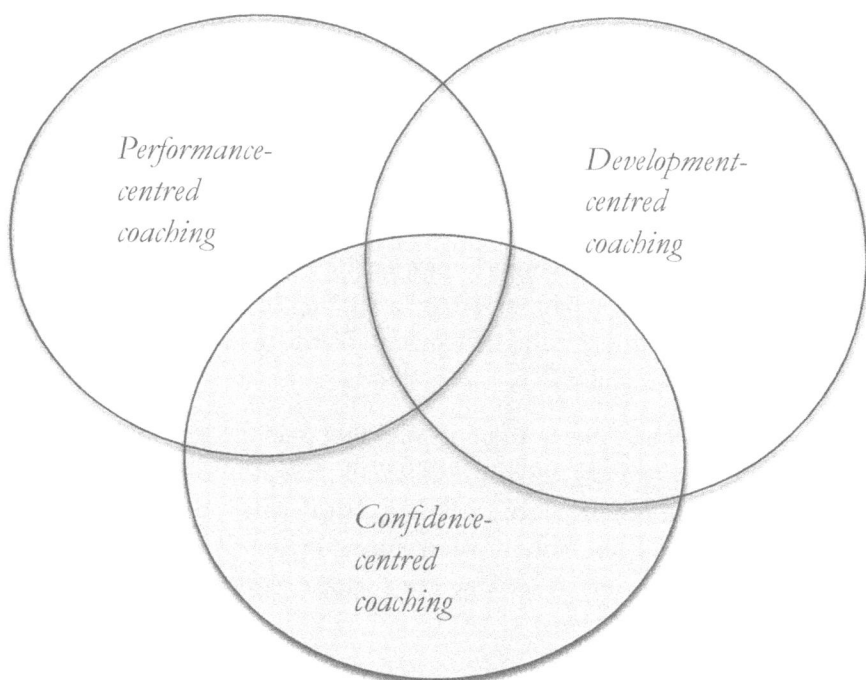

Confidence-centred:
- deeper focus on self-belief
- subjective measures of feeling, motivation and "surprising yourself with what you can do"
- deepen expertise by self-awareness, developing trusting relations and the core practices of a confidence-centred coach

Performance-centred coaching

Here the emphasis is all on hard, clearly defined goals and measures. Performance and end results are defined in narrow objective terms: peaking for specific events, fast times, final scores and wins and losses, podium places. Here's where you will hear the business-inspired mantra "If you can't measure it, you can't manage it." In triathlon, like many other sports, we see increasingly data-driven approaches: training prescribed and assessed against heart rate zones, power output on the bike, measures of lactate build-up and tolerance.

And if I want to deepen a performance-centred coaching practice, I would need to go further into the underlying science, to evidence-based research to seek out ever more rigour to achieve finite improvements. Similarly, in other sports we might think of the best coaches as the ones displaying the most advanced, empirically proven fitness programmes, the most analytical, precise attention to every detail affecting end results or sharpest tactical acumen.

And just as an aside, in elite, professional sports should an athlete or player have an issue with confidence or motivation, it is likely to be seen through the lens of how it affects their performance. Best pack them off to another scientifically orientated expert, a Sports Psychologist, to get them analysed, prescribed with a well-researched formula to fix the problem and have them back performing as required.

In case of any doubt, I am not saying a narrow performance focus doesn't have its place. I have a coaching business built, in part, on aspiring athletes wanting to achieve performance goals. All that detailed, empirically robust expert knowledge I gained on courses, through painstaking trial and error experience and continuously looking out for new evidence-based methods comes into its own. And yet…

Development-centred coaching

By contrast we have what might be thought of as development-centred coaching. When I am with a group of young triathletes or swimmers, my focus will be on a much wider objective: sharing and hoping to kindle a love for our sport, a wide open-endedness for whatever might lie ahead. In an overlap with performance-centred coaching, I want to teach certain specific skills – not for an immediate end result at the next event but to help equip and fire up a lifelong passion. In terms of measuring my success there will be an element of the young person's prowess at their newfound skill – though I'll be more concerned with whether they have fully engaged in and enjoyed the session, how active and happy they seem to be and whether they keep coming back (especially if it's in their torrid adolescence).

And how do I deepen my practice? Almost certainly it will be through finding ways of being more creative and making the sessions and learning experiences enjoyable, without necessarily a rigid right and wrong way of performing. Research from the world of education and learning[4] would direct me toward mixing things up, throwing in the unexpected – all to engage, create memorable moments and make it fun. Onlooking parents might query whether there is any method in the apparent madness. This can make for a tricky terrain of mismatched expectations to navigate, and call for extra skills on my part! But that's another book in itself.

In many coaching textbooks and courses we find these two different focal points uneasily juxtaposed. The main thrust remains all about improving performance by proven, evidence-based techniques, whilst we are also reminded to think of the person in front of us as "person first, athlete second". Yet the shape of a new way of coaching seems indistinct and unconnected to how we are taught to be coaches. In essence the centre remains grounded in performance. I think we can begin to have a more rounded, coherent, effective way of coaching if we bring in our third, overlapping focus.

Confidence-centred coaching

As in the diagram, I see a yet to be developed space for what I call confidence-centred coaching, rooted in understanding and supporting self-belief. The goals are much more subjective, emotional and deeply felt than in performance-centred coaching, with a beauty, a power and energy that (in the over-used jargon but appropriate) can be genuinely life-changing – as well as directly impacting on performance. And an open love of the sport might come, but our purpose goes beyond developmental goals to what is felt at a more personal level.

Imagine the feeling of someone coming away from a challenge that they had never quite believed themselves capable of doing. Is it just about their competitive final position, score, time? Another memorable, fun experience

---

[4] B. Busch and E. Watson *The Science of Learning: 77 studies that every teacher needs to know* (2019) is a great source of challenging received wisdom.

amongst everything else they have going on in their lives? Or the humbling, beyond belief, deeply felt wonder of somehow surprising themselves – at any level and age – with what they can do?

And what will be our guides and measures of success? For me, looking at our three domains of confidence:

- *confident coaches*:

    - it starts with my own sense of being true to myself, at ease, fluent and creative, how I feel coming away from each session, whether I have a hunger for coming back and an openness to learn from those around me

- *confidence in the coach*:

    - I'll want to focus on the quality and depth of connection with those I coach, our mutual respect and easiness as we explore creatively working together

- *coaching for confidence*:

    - whether those I coach can't quite believe what they have done and, in that way, find a new excitement and irrepressible desire to see how much further they can go.

How to develop and deepen such practice? Well, that is the purpose of this book.

Coaching in the overlap?

Now, one way of rethinking and challenging ourselves in our coaching would be to focus on the central overlap in our Venn diagram, drawing in elements of each circle as needed. If you are in a highly competitive, performance environment you are sure to be required to base much of what you do in the narrowly results-orientated, objectively measured, technical and tactical performance-centred circle – and I have no doubt that the ideas and practices to be introduced in this book around confidence and self-belief will add much to what you do. Similarly, if your main focus is more developmental in nature, perhaps working with young people or complete novices, then I believe drawing in the overlap of what follows will prove very valuable – such as when we come to look at the trusting relationships we develop, creativity and motivation.

Yet I want to suggest something way more far-reaching here, beyond borrowing useful techniques and ideas from different spheres of coaching. If I make confidence and self-belief the heart of coaching, whether working with elite performers or newcomers, everything changes. The centre shifts to a wholly different set of values and aims, skills and methods. I still want to draw on performance-centred rigour and detailed knowledge to be able to steer those I work with; and I also want to maintain a developmental sense of joyful, even playful discovery. But all with a different sense of purpose and presence, a deeper quality of connection, a different set of measures of success and skills to make my own and excel at. In short, coaching in a very different landscape – one whose key features, contours and colours we will begin to see as we set out on our journey.

So our quest is to go beyond the idea of coaching in an overlap of different spheres or circles to something deeper and more fundamental. Ask yourself: what is at the heart of your coaching, the coach you want to be (rather than the things you do), the difference you want to make? How do you want to feel in the moment of your coaching? And what is the feeling you hope those you coach will be left with? As suggested in the Preface, it's going to call for some courage to rethink much of the taken for granted assumptions about what coaches do – to ask ourselves some searching "what if…" questions.

What if our greatest skills lie not so much in instructional prowess in imparting expert knowledge as in our ability to be attuned to ourselves and those we coach? To help them (and ourselves) find an easy fluency? And all built on relationships of trust and meaningful connections? As we will see, everything changes.

Guiding stars

Now, there are several stars that will help guide us, highlighting some key principles of our new way of being. The following is as much an acknowledgement of the debt of gratitude as a way of shining some light on our path ahead and the landscape to make our own.

Belief in the person in front of us

And the first is *Carl Rogers*, the creator of person-centred therapy[5]. There is something very striking and powerful in the very term person-

---

[5] C. Rogers *On Becoming a Person: A therapist's view of psychotherapy* (2020).

centred therapy. As in the quote below, Rogers' approach was based not on positioning the therapist as the expert analyst, a detached all-knowing interpreter of a patient's innermost workings. His approach, in contrast, was founded on a fundamental belief in each person's own ability, their potential for growth and a wholeness that can only come from their own discovery of self. By removing the therapist or psychologist from the centre and instead making everything revolve around the client's way of making sense of their world, Rogers constructed a whole new approach, with different ways of working, values, principles, concepts and terms. A new landscape of therapy.

"If I can be genuinely understanding, try to listen not only to the words but to the meaning, trying to understand the person that's hidden within each of us, that's helpful.

If I really care about this person in an unconditional way, that's helpful.

If I can really be myself in the relationship – not a professional expert, not a quote 'psychologist', not a psychotherapist, just me in that relationship, that's helpful."

Carl Rogers[6]

Some powerful guiding principles for us in our coaching are there in the brief quote. "If I can be…" suggests to me a purposive, intentionally unassuming bringing of who we genuinely are to our relationships – a conscious effort to put aside any presumptions that we know best or must come up with all the answers, nor a list of things for those we coach to do.

There is also the deeply respectful looking to understand how those in front of us make sense of their world. Some Sports Psychology seems to me to lose this all-important dimension of *meaningfulness*. It is as if, in the quest to reduce everything down to cause and behavioural effect, to short lists of factors and prescriptive formulas for putting things right, we are left with sterile processes without their living subjects. Scientifically sound yet

---

[6] C. Rogers *Carl Rogers on person-centred therapy*, PsychotherapyNet (2012). Available from www.youtube.com/watch?v=o0neRQzudzw [accessed 27 September 2024].

colourless, abstract constructs devoid of the person in front of us: who they are, what they feel and how they make sense of their world.

And here is another guiding principle for our own approach: everything starts with the uniqueness of the person in front of us. One size fits all solutions, catchy top tips and other formulaic approaches will not do. We want to develop a skilful, respectful, attentive way of centring our attention on those we coach. A practical guide for sports coaches to do this – very much influenced by Carl Rogers' person-centred therapy – comes from Professor *Stephen Rollnick*, co-founder of Motivational Interviewing (MI)[7]. Stephen also happens to be a friend, mentor and source of great encouragement to me writing this book.

One idea which he and his co-authors talk about, and we will see more of in later chapters, is the "fixing reflex". As coaches we are adept at spotting what someone may be doing wrong and quickly jump in with a fix-it to put it right. As I write this I can picture myself poolside, watching a swimmer labouring through the water and gasping for air – and I'm so ready to tell them to stop and breathe in the way I know works for me and others. And yet my corrective fix-it, though without doubt technically the right one to suggest, may do little to address what the swimmer is actually feeling and what might be getting in their way. Unless, of course, I ask them. Openly, without any hint of judgement, maybe share that I can see they are struggling (if that's what they relay) and only then suggest something different for them to try. We will see more of this specific example in action and the enormously positive effect on confidence in a later chapter.

Central to MI are challenging skills that are highly relevant to our coaching. One is "uncluttered empathy". Can I put aside my preconceptions, my in the moment reactions or judgements as well as that instinctive readiness to jump in with a solution – to allow myself to be inquisitive, to wonder what's going on for this person? We will see this and other skilful MI practices in action in the book.

---

[7] S. Rollnick, J. Fader, J. Breckon and T.B. Moyers *Coaching Athletes to be Their Best: Motivational interviewing in sports* (2020); W. Miller and S. Rollnick *Motivational Interviewing: Helping people change and grow* (2024).

Belief in abilities

The next set of ideas that guided my thinking – and I know not without some controversy – come from US Social Psychologist and researcher *Carol Dweck* with her notion of growth and fixed mindsets[8]. Briefly, Carol Dweck highlighted a significant difference in how we typically approach challenging tasks, and our attitudes, self-belief (or otherwise) and assumptions about our abilities. These get reinforced, ingrained and played out in the way we talk – for example, we might say of someone that they are "gifted", "a natural" or praise their seemingly effortless ability as if it were fixed and given. Carol Dweck pointed out that this can foster a certain kind of self-confidence – up to the point when things don't work out or go right, typically leaving the person demoralized and at a loss to know why it's no longer happening for them. For many, better not to undertake the challenge than fail. In contrast, those with what she called growth mindsets typically would be animated by challenges, seeing them as worth trying for the experience rather than any anticipated or guaranteed success. Concentrated effort and focus, together with a more relaxed, less all or nothing attitude toward failure seemed to be the hallmarks of the growth mindset.

Now, Carol Dweck's work has its detractors and critics, challenging the research evidence and the wide, arguably over-reaching of its applications[9]. Stepping back from the claims and counter-claims, for me there is something enormously helpful in her idea of mindsets: the assumptions and attitudes we have about our abilities. It alerts us to how undermining and inhibiting the stories we create about ourselves can be. I recognize this in many of those who come to me for coaching (and sometimes in myself). How often do we hear someone say "I could never do that" "I'm never going to be any good at…" "I'm going to be your greatest challenge"? A self-defeating variant is when a particular suggestion they are trying out for the very first time doesn't instantly happen – "Oh, why can't I do this? I'm just being stupid."

We will see how the idea of growth and fixed mindsets can help a self-doubting athlete to slow down, be kinder to themselves and accept that learning any new skill or mastering something different to what they've been used to takes

---

[8] C. Dweck *Mindset: How you can fulfill your potential* (2012).

[9] For a detailed critique of the research evidence, see A.P. Burgoyne, D.Z. Hambrick and B.N. Macnamara 'How firm are the foundations of mind-set theory? The claims appear stronger than the evidence' in *Psychological Science*, 31(3), 258–267 (2020).

patient persistence. Sometimes simply suggesting we attach the word "yet" to those self-defeating diatribes – "I can't do this… yet" – is enough.

There's also something very pertinent for us as coaches in the idea of growth and fixed mindsets – our own openness to learning. This isn't about an accumulation of technical or tactical knowledge to bolster the doing of our coaching. It's about that same excitement, readiness to try the new and openness to the unfamiliar that Carol Dweck saw as growth mindsets. As coaches we can be rather fixed and dismissive in our thinking about what works. We probably all have an element of thinking we know better than others – how else would we put ourselves forward as coaches? But do we always model the same attitude to learning and growth that we want to see in those we coach?

And maybe we can attach the magic word "yet" when we catch ourselves dismissing a particular approach or idea – rather than "that's rubbish", "I'd never do it like that", we could adopt a more open, inquisitive "I don't understand it or see the benefit… yet."

Belief with a voice

The final set of ideas that have been very impactful and helped shape my thinking and practice come from US Performance Psychologist *Michael Gervais* and Seattle Seahawks Head Coach *Pete Carroll*[10]. I first came across Michael Gervais, speaking about the difference, as he put it, between the science and the art of coaching: the science being the technical and tactical. He went on to talk about the art of coaching – as connections and relationships, all derived from treating the person in front of us with "the highest regard." And the work with Pete Carroll at the Seahawks demonstrated that the kind of approach I was naturally drawn to was being practised in the most pressurized, high profile of sports. We will come to several ideas and practices of theirs in the following chapters: an emphasis on knowing and being able to articulate one's personal philosophy, the power of coaching moments, the creation of living masterpieces.

Here, there is another impactful idea to highlight as it leads us to another key principle. One that Pete Carroll brought to the fore: the coach as a voice for change.

---

[10] M. Gervais with P. Carroll *Compete to Create: An approach to living and leading authentically* (2019).

In the early months of the pandemic there was something of a yearning to "go back to normal", to put all the uncertainty and restrictions aside and return to the world as we knew it. If not before, certainly after the murder of George Floyd and the eruption of Black Lives Matter, more people came to realize that there was so much in the old "normal" that we should never go back to. The #MeToo movement had a similar impulse of awakening us to the unacceptability of so much that had previously been taken to be "just the way things are".

Pete Carroll stood out as one of the clearest and most passionate voices in sport about racism. He called on coaches across all sports to step up, to use their positions of influence, to stand out as a leadership group and join the voices of those who up to then had not been heard or listened to.

"No more being quiet, no more being afraid to talk to topics, no more 'Well, I'm a little uncomfortable, I might lose my job over this because I've taken a stand here or there.' Screw it. We can't do that anymore."

Pete Carroll, press conference, 29 August 2020

Uncomfortable, isn't it? Making a stand takes us out of the conventional, conveniently cosseted view of coaching: no room for anything vaguely "political" or controversial, as if we operate in a context-free environment, just coach and coached narrowly focused on our sporting endeavour. Pete Carroll's call to give voice about endemic racism goes to a truth that takes us back to that question of how we get the attention of those we coach. Whether we are conscious of it or not, our position as coaches has an influence on those around us. The question is: are we going to use that position to make a difference and be a voice for change? Or go along with and, in so doing, continue to replicate a "normal" that leaves so many unheard, without a voice, assumed not to have a place? How does this show in the way we reach out, respond and engage with others, in the language we use, in the efforts we make to really listen to what is going on for those we coach?

Now, you might think this is straying beyond a way of coaching with confidence at its centre. And yet it could not be more central. Again drawing on Pete Carroll, we will see in a later chapter that our quest to be the best coach only we can be, true to ourselves, is rooted in truly knowing and being able to articulate our values — the beliefs that we have and aim to live and coach by. How we make a stand, the difference we make, the actions we take seem to naturally follow when we are true to those beliefs and values. And here Pete Carroll emphasized that, for him and the Seattle Seahawks, it all comes down to really caring for those around him, to treating people with the utmost respect and deepest regard.

So these key principles will guide us:

- a fundamental belief in each person's potential for growth and the amazing things they can do with just the right degree of challenge, expert care and encouragement

- the uniqueness of the person in front of us and an uncluttered, inquisitive openness to understand their feelings and meaning-filled aspirations

- a deep, sensitive search for what gets in their way of discovering how great they can be

- a beliefs-driven, highly skilful art of coaching where we learn all the time from those we coach, and from pioneers and leaders in our own fields and beyond

- a consciousness to model the very behaviours and actions we hope to see in others and to make a difference.

We will come across many others who have had a big impact on my thinking, rethinking and putting into practice: some well known (such as Brené Brown on vulnerability, belonging and much more), others perhaps less well known or, one might think, unusual for a book on coaching (such as Alain de Botton on looking at art or Kae Tempest on connection). Big thanks to all.

Here be dragons

One final, brief thought about the territory we are about to enter.

This chapter opened with the idea of mapping out where we are and where we are heading. Uncomfortable though it may be, it should be said that the maps we have are somewhat sketchy, detailed in places but alongside large unexplored blanks waiting to be filled out – and some unsettling features lurking in the corners.

Instead of thinking of our map as a pinpoint accurate, detailed representation of all that lies before us, imagine the kind of early maps that intrepid sea explorers might have had as they set off on their small ships into uncharted waters. Navigating by the stars with maps that only showed the outlines of unexplored coastlines. Vast areas of the unknown and a few ominous warnings scrolled in Latin: "Here be dragons."

There is an important element of entering the unknown once we start on our quest to be the best coach only we can be – our very uniqueness (like that of those we coach) means that there isn't an already worked out map for us to follow. What follows in this book is not a ready-made, one size fits all detailed prescription of how to coach. The very nature of coaching with confidence at the centre of everything we do is one of discovering for ourselves where we are uniquely at our best: navigating our way in uncharted territories; coming to know where we can find calm; the source and qualities of energy we need; where we are at our most vulnerable and exposed; and the dragons to steer clear of and those to face.

"Sometimes you have to play a long time to be able to play like yourself."

Miles Davis

And this takes time. The same unrushed, compassionate, attentive space we want to create for those we coach – encouraging the patient persistence we touched on in relation to Carol Dweck's fixed and growth mindsets – is just as applicable to us. As in the quote from the master of cool Miles Davis, it takes dedication and purposeful perseverance to find and truly know our voice. Which leads nicely into our first Reflective Conversation.

A Reflective Conversation: Entering the space in between with Joel Enoch

This picks up the idea that we are in something of a transition from one, taken for granted world of coaching to another, yet to be clearly defined paradigm. I wanted to explore this with a coach who has direct experience of bringing their own very thoughtful, reflective, wellbeing-centred approach to an environment that might be thought of as the epitome of highly performance-orientated coaching.

I first met Joel Enoch when I was mentoring another candidate on British Triathlon's High Performing Coach Programme. In their final presentations Joel gave a very thought-provoking outline of how he saw *humility* as the grounding of great coaching practice – very much in tune with themes that have been introduced here and will be developed further: of letting go of the coach as the all-knowing expert, an openness to truly listen to and understand the person in front of us. We have maintained contact through a self-support peer group in which values and beliefs-driven coaching regularly come up. Joel was then recruited by British Cycling to lead the Paralympic Talent Development Programme. I wanted to know more about his experience of and insights from bringing his distinctive personal approach to (what I assumed would be) a highly competitive, performance-driven environment.

Lesson one: don't always assume your questions are the right ones to ask!

Defaulting to doing

Before we get there, Joel said something early on in our conversation that we didn't fully explore but I've been holding in mind. In his new position, just six months in when we talked, he was responsible for 18 Paralympic riders across a range of cycling disciplines and Paralympic categories; some with strong cycling backgrounds, others relatively new to the sport. Joel was involved in selecting each to join the Para Talent Academy: an intensive British Cycling coaching programme from which some progress on to represent Great Britain at the Paralympics and other major international competitions. It sounded daunting – and Joel admitted to feeling somewhat overwhelmed in the early days. The phrase that has stuck with me is that he found himself needing to focus on "*competence before confidence*".

It made me think of the hesitancy and uneasy feelings I can have when confronted by a new coaching challenge – and how I instinctively might revert to some notion of what I'm expected to do, as if attempting an imitation of someone who knows what they are doing. How hard to allow ourselves the space to be ourselves, doubts and all, and find an easiness and flow in our coaching. I believe this book provides a way to get there with that patient, self-compassionate persistence mentioned above. And it starts, very much as Joel went on to emphasize, from knowing and being true to ourselves.

Goals and the five whys

The idea of knowing ourselves – what Joel referred to as the "why" – was a theme in much of our conversation. For Joel, a key issue was that many athletes who enter high performance environments come to be so absorbed and focused on their lives as athletes that their whole identity revolves around their sport. Their sense of self-worth becomes tied into narrowly defined sporting achievements. Other commitments and responsibilities, such as home life, might come to be seen as something of a hindrance or distraction. And no wonder, when injuries occur or the inevitable creep of age slows them down, a big part of their "why" is thrown into doubt, leaving them feeling lost, empty and without a purpose.

Joel's view was that, to some extent, success in such competitive environments requires a single-minded obsessiveness – what we might think of as a selfishness where there is little space even for teamwork, let alone putting others outside of the sport first. Yet even in the most individual of sports, success depends to an extent on teamwork. How difficult, yet vital for the athlete's wellbeing (and those around them), to be able to intentionally choose and switch between self and other orientations. And to have the humility to recognize when the balance gets lost.

On a recent camp for the newly selected Talent Squad there was the obligatory discussion of goals – "we must have goals" being the long-received wisdom. Joel was keen to explore in more depth what he heard:

– "So what do you want to get out of the programme? Tell me about your 'why'."

– "I want to make the most of the opportunity given to me."

– "That's great – very commendable. And why?"

– "To be my best."

– "And why? What does that mean for you?"

With each more nuanced, deeper level of answer, Joel said he would be better able to steer those on the programme. On the camp there wasn't the opportunity to take these much further – to go through what Joel referred to as "the five whys", purposefully looking for deeper understanding for both the coached and coach. Like Joel on the camp, I believe such conversations are best carried out over time, as the coach and athlete come to know each other and themselves better and with enough space to dwell on what is really meaningful. If I delve through a succession of my own "whys", I also notice how my answers progressively move from short – perhaps initially rather clichéd – one-liners to more intricate, personally meaningful stories full of mixed emotions. Not to be rushed or forced.

So why all this introspection? Especially in an environment where exceptional resources are being brought to bear in the expectation of exceptional results? For Joel this centred around supporting and encouraging the riders to flourish as whole people, to help ensure their sense of worth is not tied to how far they get in their sport, exceptional and tremendously exciting though that might be. His experience has also been that there can be a freeing up from the pressure of others' expectations and judgements, when an athlete can identify what truly drives them – with amazing results following.

"By guiding the athletes to understand themselves more, their deeper meanings and motivations, they are better prepared to navigate the road of sport that lies ahead. The positive implications of this enhanced sense of self… include… resilience and patience when things are not as they would like and a deeper connection to what they love about their sport. In turn this helps steer a fulfilling and healthy career and make the tough decisions about their progress in the sport. Crucially, it also helps them redefine success away from extrinsic goals that largely lie outside their control, such as making the team or winning, and toward intrinsic motivations which can provide a lifetime of motivation, joy and flourishing."

Holism and painting

Back to my curiosity about what I had assumed would be a clash of different philosophies and approaches – and, rather predictably, turned out to be far less clear-cut.

British Cycling has stood out in the past as pioneering a philosophy of relentless improvement through so-called marginal gains. Other sports – including triathlon where I had my grounding – followed, with increasing emphasis on data-driven approaches.

Joel spoke of the realization within British Cycling that the athletes, as people, had come to be somewhat marginalized. Now the ethos is changing in British Cycling to one that is much more about creating cultures and environments (no coincidence how often these words came up in our conversation) in which athletes can thrive and grow. Other words Joel used here are informative: "flourishing", "holistic", "creative", "open", "vulnerable". At the same time he stressed "we still have to do the detail" of rigorously designed training programmes and prepare riders for peak performances which ultimately will determine how far they go. And of course some do not progress on the programme and have to make way for other, potentially higher-flying prospects. How much better to deal with such difficult, potentially life-changing decisions in a set-up that values those qualities Joel mentioned.

I wondered whether Joel had found himself caught in a mismatch of the old and new cultures – thinking of our fish and birds transition and the murky middle where a new way of being is taking shape. Interestingly Joel spoke about tentatively finding his way, initially with some compromising necessary to meet what seemed to be expected of him. Yet the impression I had was that by being clear and assured in his own beliefs and values, Joel has found he is more understanding of others and where they are coming from – and I sensed a greater confidence in his own approach as not something woolly and vague but delivering demonstrable results.

"There are certainly times when I feel a sense of pressure to fall in line. However, my feeling is that the best leaders are servants and so our job as coaches is to support people's whole personal development: neither always 'teaching' cycling nor stepping back in the name of 'athlete-led coaching'. We can do better but this takes confidence rooted in humility, to put yourself out there, try new things, learn and change tack when you get things wrong – it's okay to try and fail."

So our conversation subtly came back to confidence in coaching as grounded in knowing ourselves and the values we hold to be true. There was also a sense of an open-ended excitement and creativity in how Joel talked about the art and science of coaching. He used an image of a painter: they would need to know something of the properties of their paints, how their make-up affects application. Yet the exciting artistry comes in how the paints are brought to life, expressing the artist's deeper feelings and connection to their subjects.

Our conversation brought to life for me that, like an artist, the more connected we are to our own feelings, the more vibrant, expressive and engaging our coaching is likely to be. The art of coaching from the heart and soul.

Final words with Joel on where he sees his coaching taking him: "Rooted in faith, I want to lean into the person I have been created to become without fear."

So what are some of the key features of our new, emerging landscape that we can take in to our next chapter, where we open up and explore confidence? I think of the following:

- a commitment to finding our own, unique, true to ourselves way of coaching, as the grounding for all we do

- making confidence the heart of all we do – as what we and those we coach feel – whilst drawing in from the overlaps the precision and rigour of performance-centred coaching and the joyful playfulness of development-centred coaching

- the deeply meaningful purpose of helping those we coach surprise themselves with what they can do

- an unrushed, attentive readiness to ask ourselves and those we coach – to the extent they are open to do so – the deeper "whys" and "what else" questions

- coaching as a highly skilful, creative art, full of purpose and promise.

Time to look at what we mean by confidence and what it looks and feels like in practice.

2
Rethinking confidence

"… that strange buoyancy of the soul we call confidence."

The School of Life[11]

THIS CHAPTER OPENS up and explores confidence – the heart of our confidence-centred coaching. What is it? As coaches how can we best think of it? What does confidence look and feel like?

We will:

- see from the outset an enigmatic, paradoxical quality that is fundamental to our understanding of confidence

- explore what is really going on and what is *felt*, much of it hard to articulate in the moment

- uncover powerful ways of making the underlying feelings a central part of our coaching practice, for us as coaches and for those we coach

- capture something of the in the moment magic at play for a leading coach in the Reflective Conversation at the end of the chapter.

As always, our grounding is in people's experiences and stories, rather than abstract theory or textbook descriptions and one size fits all prescriptions.

---

[11] From The School of Life *On Confidence* (2017).

A fresh perspective on confidence

In Sports Psychology, confidence is typically defined as a self-belief and certainty of being up to the task. Positivity, resilience, a fighting spirit and ability to learn from setbacks are common themes. We need no persuading of the powerful effects of confidence on performance. But there seem to be fewer perspectives or insights into what it actually is and how it comes about in the first place: confidence as the critical factor that explains what happens but isn't explainable itself.

More generally, the way we typically talk about confidence is as a kind of x factor – a magical quality that explains why some succeed against all odds, and others fail or feel unwilling to try. For many sports coaches this leads them to see confidence and motivation as a fixed, given attribute much like physique – a "thing" you either have or you don't. And we often think we can readily spot it in others, but typically without really knowing what they are experiencing and genuinely feeling.

There is another way to think of confidence:

- as fluid and dynamic, rather than fixed, with both discernible, sometimes predictable patterns and sometimes unexpected ruptures or surprising breakthroughs

- as a complex interaction, highly influenced by others and our environment as well as deeply rooted in the individual

- a challenging and deeply rewarding area of coaching that can be opened up, understood and developed, whilst still being inherently personal and magical in its effects.

The confidence paradox

And here we start with our central paradox: that we feel a definite *absence* of confidence acutely but much less its *presence*. What does this mean? Listening to sportspeople in general and reflecting on our experiences, we instinctively know and can put into clear words the feeling of *losing* confidence. That undermining sense of being overwhelmed, emptied out and unable to get anything right. Such and such happened "and I just lost all my confidence". Or we might think we see it, all too painfully clear as a footballer steps up for their turn in a penalty shoot-out – an almost infectious unease of someone about to blow it.

Yet I don't think the same is true for *having* confidence. Would we say we "have confidence" or "are confident" with the same degree of clear, definite certainty? Indeed, when someone says they are confident and sure of themselves facing a sporting challenge, we might wonder whether that's coming from a misplaced arrogance – or maybe the challenge is not actually so great! And in truth we have no idea what is really going on for someone who we might think "looks confident".

I believe that what we might take to be confidence is actually felt and rooted in three other, deeper emotions: excitement, control and fluency. And I believe we can coach for these.

Excitement

There's a super book by the extraordinary Brownlee brothers, called *Swim Bike Run*[12], that recounts each of their stories, side by side, to becoming triathlon Olympic and World Champions. It opens with their accounts, moment by moment, of waking up, heading out and lining up at the start of their epic 2012 London Olympic race where they went on to finish first and third. Interestingly, nowhere does the word "confidence" appear. Nor is there any hint of that supposed "certainty" in standard definitions of confidence. Instead, what comes through is an extraordinary sense of excitement, just to be there, in that moment.

> "Instantly I felt the excitement. Never before have I felt like that on the morning of a race; usually there are nerves. You are shaky, you struggle to eat breakfast. This morning there was none of that. It was pure excitement."
>
> Alistair Brownlee in *Swim Bike Run*

It is worth saying that this kind of energizing excitement doesn't seem to be overly focused on a strong likelihood of medals or other rewards, waiting to be captured at the end – though I'm sure both brothers would, at times, have visualized themselves on the podium. What I see in the Brownlees' stories, in the athletes I've coached for major challenges and my own (albeit not as heady) experience is more an exhilarating sense of "how brilliant to

---

[12] A. Brownlee and J. Brownlee with T. Fordyce *Swim Bike Run: Our triathlon story* (2014).

be here", a part of what is about to unfold, revelling in the energy of each moment and a thrilled anticipation about what lies ahead, whatever that might hold.

> "At a stroke my final nerves went. I looked at the endless smiling faces, felt the cheers hammering my ears and thought: this is the coolest thing I've ever experienced."
>
> Jonny Brownlee in *Swim Bike Run*

How to do this? Being in a high energy environment obviously can help (though equally can be totally overwhelming and undermining). More fundamental is how we conceive of the challenge ahead: what will count as a brilliant, successful experience; and what we seek out and nurture. One way I have found helpful for many of the triathletes, swimmers and other endurance sportspeople I've coached is what we call *bringing the finish line to the start*. In other words, instead of letting the times, positions or final scores at the end define success, we first allow ourselves to celebrate and feed off the excitement of being at the start line. All that training done. The moment has arrived. We are here and, like the Brownlees, relishing the sheer excitement of being wholly present.

And from there, we think of the space between the start and finish as an empty canvas where we will create, what Michael Gervais and Pete Carroll term, *our living masterpiece*. Each moment in that space becomes a chance to express ourselves at our very best. Times and places have a way of taking care of themselves as we surprise ourselves with what we can do.

In later chapters we will explore how to seek out and nurture this sense of thrilled anticipation: being wholeheartedly present, completely focused on the space ahead and the chance to create our own living masterpiece.

Control and uncertainty

A second defining, deeper element in the confidence mix is the sense of being prepared and on top of those things we can control – and at the same time being aware of and at ease with those things we can't.

You will probably recognize control as a much more common theme in the standard approaches to confidence. We will see in Chapter

7 on motivation that one of the most influential approaches, Self-Determination Theory[13], gives special weight to realizing a degree of autonomy – the sense that one's actions determine or control what happens, that we are in charge.

Here there is an obvious place for what, in the previous chapter, we called the performance-centred work of a coach in preparing those we coach for their events and competitions – of being meticulous about every aspect of their training and preparation. For those athletes I coach, we aim for them to stand at the start line and know they are as well prepared as they could possibly be – and then let whatever happens unfold. We identify, think through and rehearse every detail that will have an impact – for example, if it's a triathlon, getting to the start, registering, setting up the transition space, currents and tides, the bike and run terrain, likely conditions, kit, nutritional requirements and more. Our goal, however, goes deeper than the obvious impacts on performance, the cumulative effect of all those so-called marginal gains, key though these are. Above all, we are after *a stilling, calming composure.*

And in this respect, control is only half the story. Being aware of and developing an acceptance of those things we cannot control, able to acknowledge and accept those things we can't do much about allows us to let go of anxiety. And at the same time we want to prioritize those things where our positive energy and focus are best placed.

In this respect we are a long way from the kind of controlling, somewhat obsessive dictating of detail one sees in micro-managers or those who must have everything done their way. One suspects their desire for control actually comes from a deep-seated sense of insecurity and lack of control. They may project an aura of confidence and assertiveness, but one wonders how deep this goes – and what effect their controlling behaviour has on others around them.

So our confidence mix at one and the same time holds an excitement and thrilled anticipation together with a calming, composed readiness for what lies ahead. And it is into that space, the blank canvas ahead and the living masterpiece waiting to be created, that we now move with our third element.

---

[13] E.L. Deci and R.M. Ryan *Intrinsic Motivation and Self-Determination in Human Behavior* (1985).

Fluency

Here's where the magical part underpinning confidence comes in – the sense of being so absorbed, body and mind in tune with the moment, as to lose and find ourselves in whatever activity we are engaged in. Let's step back in time to illustrate what can happen to fluency and its effect on confidence when it all goes wrong.

I can picture it now, even though it was over 40 years ago. The County 5km Championship and I was as fit and well prepared as I'd ever been. There were some national-level stars lining up at the start line, with me just outside the likely medals but excited and ready for a super-competitive, fast race. From the gun a blistering pace was set, with me tucked in to just the right position, composed and poised for the best 5km of my life. Or so I thought.

A few laps in and it wasn't just the leading stars who started moving out of reach. Surprisingly another club member, who I would have expected to leave far behind, was now striding out, looking strong and getting further away from me. And with each stride I became acutely aware of how hard I was having to run; how much my calves hurt; how tensed up I was; what a struggle to get in enough air; how I just couldn't go any faster. In my head I was already thinking about how others would see my poor performance, defining it for myself as such even before the end. I was rehearsing what I might say by way of explanation (not that I could find any, hard as I thought). And as the painful laps went by I found myself playing out a conversation to convince myself that it would be worse to drop out than to finish in a disappointing time and place.

Now, as it happens, I actually ran quite a good time, just a few seconds off what was later my fastest ever. So not quite such a disaster as I felt. But what a painful, disappointing, laboured experience!

So when I think of fluency, it is not just as a smooth execution of a particular movement. My sad and sorry tale shows the full-scale opposite of fluency: *physically* tensing up, conscious of every ache and pain and really struggling to keep going; *mentally* distracted, weighed down by thought, already writing the story of a failure and thinking ahead to the end that can't come soon enough. In contrast, the kind of fluency I seek out and want to nurture involves an almost unconscious, thought-free easiness with *mind and body in sync*. There is obviously effort, but not driven by effort-filled thinking. "It just happens." And as we will see, the *perception of time* changes.

W. Timothy Gallwey, in *The Inner Game of Tennis*[14], captures the sense of finding a harmony between body and mind, of being immersed in "a flow of action", uninhibited by over-thinking and over-trying; instead the "mind is so concentrated, so focused, that it is *still*. It becomes one with what the body is doing… without interference from thoughts."

There is also a *joy* in fluency: of everything coming together; of feeling so absorbed in the immediacy of each movement and effort that there is no space for distractions; feeling that you simply couldn't be anywhere else in that moment, totally present and right at the edge of your best – and going beyond it. The pain of pushing oneself to the absolute limit would still be there but, if anything, act as a spur to keep going, solely focused on the space just ahead. Finishing times and places tend to come as a pleasant surprise, almost an extra to the feeling that we could not have gone any better, stronger, smoother, faster… wishing it had carried on, even though every last drop of energy was expended in getting to the end. (I've felt this too!)

This all chimes with Hungarian Psychologist Mihaly Csikszentmihalyi's notion of *flow*[15]. As in the quote below, there is something hugely compelling in the idea of flow as everything coming together in the moment, a feeling of invincibility as he describes it, all distractions fading away as we "master the moment".

"Your perception of time warps as your attention narrows to the task in hand. This attention is so strongly focused on the task that all extraneous thoughts and anxieties disappear… Despite feeling invincible, you are aloof to what others think of you as your self-consciousness recedes into the background. All that matters is mastering the moment."

Mihaly Csikszentmihalyi, Philip Latter and Christine Weinkauff Duranso[16]

---

[14] W. Timothy Gallwey *The Inner Game of Tennis: The ultimate guide to the mental side of peak performance* (2015).

[15] For a sports-specific treatment: S.A. Jackson and M. Csikszentmihalyi *Flow in Sports: The keys to optimal experiences and performances* (2019).

[16] M. Csikszentmihalyi, P. Latter and C. Weinkauff Duranso *Running Flow* (2017).

In some discussions of flow there is an implication that it is an almost random state that one might be lucky to experience but cannot be willed into existence. Certain conditions need to be in place for sure, as if clearing the way for the elusive magic to happen – or not happen. There are certainly no simple formulas, top tips or tricks to conjure up the state of flow or fluency we hope our athletes will enjoy. However, we will see in Chapter 5: Coaching for confidence that it is possible to help our athletes become attuned to and able to go to this kind of fluency and flow, losing and finding themselves at their best in the moment.

And what of fluency as an in the moment, "without interference from thoughts" flow in our own coaching? Can the same happen when we are in the act of coaching? And excitement and control? We will see throughout the book many ideas and insights cross over and apply both to those we are coaching and to ourselves as coaches. So what would the paradox of confidence and deeper emotions point us to if we are reflecting on what we do as coaches?

What is felt as confidence in our coaching

I am sure we have all felt the *lack* of confidence – the feeling of emptiness or freezing in the moment when starting something very new, confronted by the totally unexpected or where we feel we have absolutely no relevant expertise, yet are still required to perform. Remember Joel's *competence before confidence*? Perhaps with experience we come to know how best to avoid situations where such feelings take over – by having well thought through plans, educating ourselves about certain areas of coaching to fill gaps in our expertise or maybe simply sticking to our so-called "comfort zones". Or maybe we just become good at hiding from others (and ourselves) our real fears of being exposed.

Now imagine if our coaching was rooted in a *conscious seeking out and nurturing* of the three underpinning feelings that lie at the heart of what we take to be confidence:

- the *excitement* experienced as a thrilled anticipation of what lies ahead, of not quite knowing what we can do as coaches, nor the person we are coaching, and being animated by the opportunity to discover how good that might be, our living masterpiece waiting to be created

- a sense of *control* experienced as a stilling, calming composure, born of being well prepared whilst also alive to and at ease with those things we can't anticipate or plan for

- *fluency* experienced as an in the moment finding and losing ourselves, where our coaching action is thought-free, instinctive and totally in tune with who we are and with the person or people we are coaching.

Doesn't that sound good – coaching with a depth and richness that would keep us motivated and wanting to discover more?

In this respect, it is worth dwelling on a theme that will come up again throughout the book: a *letting go*. Here lies another shift away from convention to a very different way of being. To find and lose ourselves at our very best requires an element of letting go of the very things that we would typically think of as the basis of our expertise, the things that give us our authority and status as coaches. And yet in the letting go there is an immense power and positive effect on us and those we coach.

Taking our three core elements underpinning what we take to be confidence, letting go might mean the following:

- *excitement*: a letting go of how we typically measure and judge success and what others seem to value, instead allowing ourselves to have an excited sense of anticipation and curiosity about what will happen in the space for our living masterpieces, revelling in the moment – and letting the results take care of themselves. In this way, we are also likely to find that there is just as much excitement, joy and satisfaction in coaching a complete novice as there is in coaching an elite or professional athlete

- *control*: as already discussed, a letting go of an anxiety about those things we can't plan for or control. Here's where the undermining "imposter syndrome" can creep in, making us feel that we must be seen as on top of everything. How liberating if we can be open and honest with ourselves and others about the uncertainties, the questions without answers and those things outside of our control. This is what Brené Brown would call our vulnerability: "having the courage to show up and be seen when we have no control over the outcome"[17]. Vulnerability not as weakness but, as she says, our greatest measure of courage

---

[17] B. Brown *Rising Strong* (2015).

- *fluency:* and this is perhaps the most radical letting go, what I call "who owns the right way?" If I am aiming to instil in the athletes I coach a fluency, where everything just seems to flow and be in balance, then how they feel becomes way more important than how they look to me or to anyone else watching from the sidelines, no matter how expert we might be. We will see more of this in practice in Chapter 5: Coaching for confidence. For now, hold this thought: who owns the right way – the coach or the athlete?

Schön's reflective practitioners

Staying with us as coaches for this final section, there is an interesting parallel here with a pioneering study by Donald A. Schön[18] of how professionals think in action. Schön analysed how architects, psychotherapists and other professionals made decisions and problem solved in their very different practices. He sought to debunk the notion of a mechanical, formulaic application of expert knowledge to the problems or challenges before them – what he termed Technical Rationality that, at the time (and arguably still today) was the dominant professionals' educational model. Instead he saw something far more creative, instinctive and tacit – many professionals unable to articulate why they came up with a particular solution, design or insight. He termed this Reflection in Action, emphasizing "the irreducible element of art in professional practice" and that "our knowing is *in* our action".

I like to think "knowing in action" could not be a better expression of the way I want to be in the coaching moment – so absorbed in the athletes or athlete before me, instinctively feeling my way to what will and won't work as if without a thought, spontaneously coming up with creative things to try that both of us learn from. And then going home wondering "Now where did that come from?"

"know-how is in the action... There is nothing... to make us say that know-how consists of rules or plans which we entertain in the mind prior to action. Although we sometimes think before acting, it also true that in much of *the spontaneous behaviour of skilful practice we reveal a kind*

---

[18] D.A. Schön *The Reflective Practitioner: How professionals think in action* (2013).

of knowing which does not stem from a prior intellectual operation."

Donald A. Schön (emphasis added)

Yet so much of the way we are trained to be coaches leans back to a model of our practice being about the application of regimented, rule-bound ways of doing things – what looks like a proper swim stroke, how to control a ball with one touch, pull on an oar, put a spin on a backhand, the tactics to employ against a certain move or team – which we're then tutored to pass on, following prescribed steps and processes, to our athletes. We are told "Of course, one may need to make certain adaptions for different people and circumstances." Fair enough.

But it is the very fact that everyone is different and that no circumstances are the same – ever – that needs to be our starting point. So-called "adaptions" are the very space in which we practise our art, learn through reflecting on "knowing in action" and, without looking for it, find an easiness and flow. We might even look back and call it "confidence".

The next chapter delves deeper into what it means to be a self-confident coach. For now, as a taster of what is to come and an insightful example of knowing in action and fluency, here are some highlights from a fascinating conversation with a leading triathlon and swim coach.

Reflective Conversation: In the moment with Kate Offord

Kate Offord is an award-winning triathlon and swim coach; founder of a very successful, distinctive coaching business; a Senior Coach Educator; and much more. She and I qualified together on the most advanced triathlon coaching programme and keep in regular touch, sharing the ups and downs of establishing and growing our private businesses, leading and letting go of Head Coach roles in large clubs and embarking on new challenges.

The following actually distils two separate, in-depth conversations we had – one a few years ago for a podcast I put together on confidence and women in coaching, with insights from Kate's coaching journey; the other, more recently, exploring some of the ideas in this chapter (without any leading prompts from me!), focused on her feelings around confidence in coaching.

Confidence as calmness

In our more recent conversation I asked Kate to think about moments in her coaching when everything seems to be going well and, in contrast, moments when it just doesn't happen or she feels unsure of herself. What is going on for her and what does she feel?

Interestingly, the very first thing she talked about was a sense of **calm** when she's in her element – an unhurried composure that she feels in herself and also passes on to others. Some of this, she said, comes from knowing she's well prepared for each session: has done the basics of any safety needs and given thought to the people coming, where they're at in a programme, the central focus or purpose of each session and ideas for what might work.

She went on to talk about how this preparedness enables her to know instinctively in the moment "when to bend and flex", adapting the sessions as needed and seizing on sudden, unconventional ideas. She gave a lovely example of animating a group of initially weary swimmers by asking them to each think of the qualities of one of their most skilful peers, to describe it in three words and then each swimmer to practise those particular qualities they had highlighted. None of which was pre-planned. All completely centred around each swimmer's perceptions and aspirations (rather than following her command). And interestingly, she said it probably wouldn't work again if she tried to replicate it.

Trusting our judgement

We also talked about the dominance of data-driven coaching in our sports and how that can make us more conscious of the basis of our own self-belief as coaches. No surprise: neither one of us looks at data in isolation nor thinks that the key to unlocking someone's potential lies in delving deeper and deeper into technical analysis or science-based measures (helpful though they may be). I know, in my case, I sometimes felt exposed, as if I was about to be found wanting in some area that others would assume every coach "should" be an authority on. Kate shared how, similarly, sometimes an athlete she is working with might approach her for a precise and definite answer to their concerns that particular "numbers" aren't as good as they believe they should be – such as their power readings on the bike – taking her into territory that, like me, she knows is unlikely to hold all the answers.

How do we communicate that to the person who makes a gadget on their wrist the arbiter and judge of good or bad performance? With experience, Kate has come to feel more at ease about stepping back from how the athlete or others perceive their "problem", to trust her judgement and ability to look at what she called "the bigger picture" – to find out and explore what other factors might be at play, beyond a narrow focus on one set of finite measures.

Thinking back to this part of our conversation, I'm struck by two things. First, how a relentless focus on narrowly defined measures and data might give a veneer of certainty to the coach and their athlete – yet crowd out the very space for deeper and broader reflections that we know are key to sustained self-belief and, in the end, incredibly rewarding, surprising performances. And secondly, how Kate's trust in her own judgement seems to sit alongside the calmness, the unhurried composure that she first highlighted as what she feels when at her best – as if calm and trust in her judgement form a virtuous circle.

Kate also talked about moments when she can feel under pressure and finds herself doubting her judgement – notably when challenged by parents about the progress of her young swimmers. She recalled being put on the spot by assertive parents, demanding she justify objectively why their child hasn't been moved up a group. As so much of what is happening in the moment poolside focuses on the children in her charge, it is as if she instinctively knows what will be best for each young swimmer – without making a front of mind, conscious weighing up of every factor. Exactly *knowing in action*, discussed above.

But how to explain such instinctive judgement calls to someone pressing for hard evidence (not that it's likely to satisfy them even if instantly to hand)? Kate said she can be left worrying that her apparent inability to articulate precise and objective reasons will be taken as her being "wishy-washy" and lacking certainty and confidence in her judgement. Yet she is actually coming from a place of being so attuned to the needs of the swimmers before her – of trusting in her instinct, and knowing in action as well as openness – that it allows her to question herself and learn. An interesting conundrum.

A quick note: beware the *fixing reflex*! Allow yourself to take in what that might feel like. Sit with the contrast of being lost in the moment of fluent coaching then suddenly being confronted and one's judgement called into question. No jumping to solutions – see if you can stay with what that kind of dilemma might feel like rather than going straight to what you might do.

Women in the coaching space

One final set of reflections and insights, these from our conversation about women in coaching and confidence a few years ago. I don't believe things have changed much since then, but at the time Kate put her finger on a pervasive, male-orientated culture within coaching in our sport. When we talked she had just come from tutoring a group of would-be Level 2 coaches, made up of 14 men and just two women. More generally, her experience has been that athletes in a club will typically expect the male coach to be taking the lead, regardless of the fact that he may be less experienced and qualified – or that the lead female coach has prepared the session. More subtly, the qualities we tend to associate with conventional coaches lean heavily toward male stereotypes.

As an aside, I think of the most popular triathlon magazine, each month packed with top takeaway tips from coaches – without exception every one of them male. Each adopts a similar pose: arms folded, authoritative stance, unemotional stare at the camera. The few expert women occasionally featured are from the supposed softer margins of nutrition or psychology – not real coaches like us blokes!

I asked about what she typically sees in the women who attend courses she runs. Too often she sees an almost apologetic hesitancy, despite them being strong women in other fields. "A lot of women don't appreciate that they are not being pushy or arrogant and have no need to apologize when they move into the coaching space." And what they do in that space need not follow the stereotypical, "loud, shouty" male model.

Kate talked about the implicit presumption many women hold that if "you can't shout, you can't be heard". Instead, she emphasized that women need to use the coaching space in a different way. For her part she said she consciously uses a mix of body language, silence and being deliberately quieter to get the athletes' attention and then their focus and engagement. "Because we're not as physical in terms of presence or a voice, we have to have different ways to be heard."

I asked Kate how we might attract more women into coaching and to discover for themselves their space and voice. Her answer – just like Joel in our previous Reflective Conversation – started essentially with self-awareness. She talked about women first working out who they are and what they want to be – and then how to portray that in their coaching. She also highlighted an acceptance that not every coaching style will fit everyone, without that undermining or undervaluing ourselves.

Final words with Kate: "I'm now confident in my coaching space – I know what my values are. I know the sort of people who share my values. And I can tailor my coaching to best fit. Having the conviction about what you know is invaluable."

So, some key ideas that strike me and that we can take into Part 2 and the next chapter on how we can develop and build our self-confidence as coaches:

- grounding our quest for confidence – our own as coaches and of those we coach – in what is felt before the words

- confidence not so much as a supposed certainty of success or being "up to the task" (as the psychology textbooks suggest), more as an excitement, experienced as a thrilled anticipation about what might lie ahead

- the calm composure that we said is another of our underlying feelings of confidence, rooted in preparedness and a readiness to adapt, "bend and flex" in the uncertain moment, also feeds in and is fed by trust in our judgement

- knowing in action as being at our most fluent, spontaneous and creative, though sometimes hard to rationalize or articulate to others

- and key to making our home within the new landscape of coaching, finding our own individual voice, uniquely ours and rooted in what we believe and want to be.

Part 2
Into three domains of confidence

3
Confident coaches

"An artist is about to enter the stage…"

S O FAR WE have outlined some key principles for all we do, challenging ourselves to think afresh about our coaching and the place of confidence at the heart of great coaching practice. From there, in the last chapter we explored what confidence can look and feel like, suggesting that what we *see* as confidence and what is actually *felt* can be two very different things. And by starting from the felt experience, we begin to open up a very different, creative and rewarding vision of coaching.

Building on this, in this chapter we will:

- explore our own confidence and self-belief as coaches, to find our unique individual voice, to know and be true to ourselves

- make three trips to a swimming pool for lessons in self-awareness, openness and how to step into and feel assured in the coaching space

- see something of this quest to find ourselves at our best in our Reflective Conversation at the end of the chapter.

Before getting going, you might think coaches' self-confidence is only relevant to those fairly new to coaching. However, even the most experienced coaches will also face moments of self-doubt and uncertainty. For me, I know at times I can be hesitant and unsure of myself. As we will see, there is much in the principles and practices explored in this chapter that is just as relevant to the very experienced as to new coaches. Indeed, some of those who are the furthest along their coaching journeys may find this part of the book the hardest to take in and act on.

Starting point: Being yourself

Here goes.

Our self-confidence as coaches starts with *knowing and being true to ourselves* – not some notion of what an ideal coach should do or be like; not the high profile, widely respected coaches of elite athletes or professional sportspeople, inspiring though some are; not the coaches around us who we might admire as role models and aim to emulate. As in the often used phrase, it's about being *the best that only you can be*.

It's very common to see lists of what a coach should do, the various roles they might play or key practices to follow. Social media is also full of sound bites of elite coaches and managers: short snippets capturing their philosophies, mantras or lessons for us to follow – some inspiring, others perhaps more questionable. Are any relevant to you, though – to the person you uniquely are and want to be?

And here's the thing: for most of us, discovering what the best only we can be is, knowing and being true to ourselves isn't as easy or obvious as it might seem. First, it takes a dedicated, sometimes uncomfortable effort at deep reflection: asking ourselves what really drives us; recognizing the implicit beliefs and preconceptions that shape how we view the world and others; having a clear sense of the values we hold and consistently applying these in how we are with others. It also means an honesty about what we feel in the moment, what touches us and evokes a reaction.

Second, we have something of a moving target. We never reach a point of complete self-awareness. Every encounter and experience, each new challenge, every interaction with others: all potentially shape our thinking – sometimes so subtly as to be unconscious, other times fundamentally challenging us to think afresh about what we believe to be important and how we want to be. And if not, why not?

Third, we typically coach in noisy, frenetic, high energy environments. There are strong expectations and preconceptions about how we should be. Finding ourselves and being true to our beliefs in such arenas is not always easy. Here lies another one of the book's interesting paradoxes. In the previous chapter we looked at *knowing in action* – being so in the flow of our coaching as to be able to instinctively respond, to spontaneously and without front of mind thought and words come up with creative ideas to try. To know and be true to ourselves calls for something that is also instinctive, that feels genuine and right in the moment and comes before the words – a *knowing in the stillness*.

"The quieter I became, the more I heard."

Erling Kagge[19]

This is what the Norwegian explorer and writer Erling Kagge alludes to as discovering the silence in ourselves. Fortunately, it doesn't take a solo trip across the Antarctic to find this silence, though immersing ourselves in nature certainly can help. Even in the most hectic and pressured moments he suggests we can find that stillness, grounding ourselves in an inner calm as if slowing down time and shutting out every distraction. As we will see in the next section, how we articulate and give voice to the person we are and want to be has a very important place, but the words come a little later, after listening to ourselves in the stillness and silence.

Why does it matter?

Now, you may be thinking "Why all this introspective stuff – can't we just get on and do what coaches do and coach?" But pause a moment: how can we truly listen to those we are coaching, and take in and understand where they are coming from, if we never make the time to listen to ourselves, sit with silence, reflect on and take in where we are coming from?

And there's something of a ripple effect. Knowing ourselves brings a calm stillness, a quietening and letting go of all the noise of expectations and rush that we all too easily get caught up in – and is somehow perceptible and transmissible to others. We will see knowing ourselves in the stillness is also key to uncluttering our minds and being able to put aside judgements and "the fixing reflex"[20] we touched on in the first chapter.

---

[19] E. Kagge, (translated by B.L. Crook) *Silence in the Age of Noise* (2018).
[20] For lots of instructive examples of this in practice: W.R. Miller and S. Rollnick *Motivational Interviewing: Helping people change and grow* (2023).

The ripples also reach across to the trust others have in us. Self-awareness is about being genuine, honest with ourselves and sure of what we believe in. We intuitively pick up on those who are "faking it" for effect – whether for ulterior motives and their own agendas, to perform what they think is appropriate to their role, or to be popular. None of these are much of a foundation for the trusting relationships we want to develop with our athletes.

And note: reflective and constantly evolving self-awareness, stillness and authenticity are not the usual stuff of your typical training course to qualify as a coach, are they? On some developmental courses we may be encouraged to think about our coaching philosophies – though it continues to surprise me how few coaches at the elite or professional level are able to clearly, meaningfully and with a genuine conviction say what theirs are. For some, their so-called philosophies, though vigorously espoused, appear to float on the surface of tactics and methods. For others they appear more like catchy phrases or marketing straplines, rather than being intimately connected to who they are and what they genuinely believe.

Knowing your values

To help us arrive at something more meaningful that will ground us in being our very best, let's make the first of our three visits to the swimming pool. Leave the coaching hat behind for now – we're still working on our own self-awareness and beliefs. And we'll take along with us, tucked in with our swimming kit, Professor Steven Peters' book *The Chimp Paradox*[21].

In it he uses a set of simple images to explain the complexities of the brain and how our minds work. As he outlines, when things happen to us, the first part of the brain to react – the amygdala in the limbic system – is like an emotive chimp: defensive, territorial, angry. What he calls the more human, reasoning parts of the brain – in and around the frontal cortex – work more by logic, by weighing up facts and past experiences and by an effort to understand others.

Now, there I am: in the pool, getting into my early morning swim, head a bit cluttered with all the things to be done that day and feeling pressed for time. In my lane (note the description, as if I owned the place!) is a slower swimmer

---

[21] S. Peters *The Chimp Paradox* (2012).

who keeps setting off ahead of me just as I am about to turn, push off the wall and zip ahead. My chimp-like territorial instincts kick in. I get angry at their lack of pool etiquette (in other words, getting in my way). I even find myself dismissively critiquing their style. I can sense myself tensing up, and my swimming becomes more aggressive, bordering on belligerent.

One of Steve Peters' ideas that I've found has a powerful effect in these very moments is what he calls the Life Stone – being clear about our values and the person we truly want to be (as if inscribed on a tablet of stone).

Pete Carroll and Michael Gervais similarly emphasize the importance of being able to articulate your philosophy – your true way of being – in less than 20 words. In their *Compete to Create* audiobook[22], they suggest a process that starts with making a list of the people we most admire – past, present, little known by others or world famous. From there, think about what it is about each one that draws us to them, digging deeper through the layers. On the surface I might really admire a particular person who is often profiled in the news or thought of highly by others. So I ask myself to look deeper at what it might be – amongst all the other high profile, outwardly successful people – that attracts me to them. Then I look at the full list to see what common themes or distinctive qualities emerge. For some on my list it might be that they seem to share a calm dignity and sense of a life lived in tune with their values. A strong moral compass that seems to be at the heart of all they do. For others, there might be a different theme of an ability to express heartfelt emotions in their art or music with an apparent fluency and depth of feeling. Or a pioneering spirit, not accepting the status quo and instead pursuing better ways of being with a restless energy.

I won't detail the full *Compete to Create* process here – though I strongly recommend it as a guide to delving into the person you truly are and want to be. What strikes me is that, by making the space to deeply reflect on qualities that touch us, something that starts with thinking of others I admire can lead to a deep sense of my own values, the things that I would want to be known for when I am at my best. It also feels far more real and meaningful than an exercise in identifying so-called strengths and weaknesses – who I am and want to be when I'm in my element rather than a checklist of things to keep doing or to stop. And I've found this is where the words come in to

---

[22] M. Gervais with P. Carroll *Compete to Create: An approach to living and leading authentically* (2019).

their own: being able to articulate these values in just a few words can have a powerful, stilling effect in the heat of a pressurized moment.

For example, one part of my own personal philosophy is "to seek out and nurture calmness". I want to feel at ease and peace with myself (having not always known this). I'll look for and cherish the company of others who share a similar way of being. And I'll want to pass on to others the same unhurried, calming sense of being listened to and attentively held.

Back in the pool, and in those chimp-like moments of reacting to other swimmers who dare intrude on my jungle path, I can bring to mind that the rush of aggression and tension isn't me – not the calm person I want to be nor the feeling I want to pass on to others. And it's worth adding, it also gently reminds me that the problem may not be so much the people around me as my reaction to them.

So even if you have a well worked phrase or summary of your coaching philosophy, I encourage you to make time to "do the work" (as Brené Brown would say): stilling yourself first to reflect on what is important to you; working through a model like the *Compete to Create* one to dig deeper into the kind of person that genuinely feels like you at your best; and then carving it, in less than 20 words, into your Life Stone.

Openness

A further set of thoughts: to be the very best coach only you can be requires an openness – to not accept our first reactions or go with preconceptions; a state of mind or readiness to learn; and to acknowledge that we don't have all the answers; that expansive technical knowledge and expertise are not enough.

There is yet another paradox here that many coaches and those involved in coach development are recognizing and that is a distinctive feature of the new landscape we are feeling our way toward. It is that a self-awareness of our doubts and uncertainties, an ability to recognize the limits of what we know, a readiness to admit we don't have all the answers – what Brené Brown calls our vulnerability[23] and others might refer to as humility – is at the heart of being the best coach only each of us can be.

---

[23] The classic TED Talk: B. Brown *The Power of Vulnerability* TED Conferences (2010). Available from: www.ted.com/talks/brene_brown_the_power_of_ vulnerability?subtitle=en [accessed 13 September 2024]

In the previous chapter we dwelt briefly on the courage of *letting go* – of being ready to see and position ourselves as not the expert imparting our knowledge to athletes, but as skilled in creating spaces in which the athletes we coach discover "the right way" for themselves and explore the outer limits of their possibilities. Above all, this calls for openness and curiosity – as outlined in practice below.

Before that, it's worth noting that those coaches who appear supremely confident and sure of themselves may actually have quite closed minds: stuck with the way they have always done things and fixed on what they require of those who come to them. The openness that we want to cultivate is certain to mean we are far more likely to empathize and be alongside those we coach; to have an intuitive feel for what will bring out the best in each of our athletes and in ourselves. And we are more likely to stay fresh, to continue learning and finding exciting, rewarding challenges.

As coaches we tend to be black and white in our views, fixed on the ways of coaching we believe in and dismissive of others. In the triathlon coaching world we see new ideas, techniques and technologies come into fashion and be taken up enthusiastically as the only way to go... until the next innovation or (sometimes not so novel) idea comes along. I wonder what gets lost along the way: the chance to challenge ourselves with different ways of thinking and perspectives; a recognition that we don't have to be expert in everything? And how tiring it must be to position oneself as the keeper of what is right and wrong.

Self-confidence and openness in practice

And so on to another visit to the swimming pool. This time picture yourself accompanying me to a one-to-one session with a disabled child (one of the things I do alongside coaching).

All around there are busy, noisy lessons going on, classes of young children boisterously splashing and more or less following their teachers' bellowed instructions. Imagine that we are due to meet for the first time a child – we are only told their name and age before we meet and know nothing more about them (as often happens). A child appears, with a noticeable disability, aided to poolside by one of their parents. Other children and adults around us are staring uneasily at the child and us, as if almost questioning why we're there. The child has a mixed look of excitement and nervousness as we make eye contact.

Now, I'll reveal what might go through my head in that instant. I might instinctively feel quite incapable, a sinking feeling of being out of my depth (keeping the watery imagery going) and a desperate "What am I going to do?" springing to mind. I might also feel moved, a pang of heartfelt sympathy as I take in the extent of their disability. And the analytical part of me might hastily scramble down a path of trying to identify the term for the child's disability and what it might typically mean for what they won't be able to do.

So what has happened in that instant? Essentially I have had a series of what I think of as *closed reactions*. I have instantly closed down and thrown into doubt my own ability. My self-confidence has momentarily left the building. And to all intents and purposes I have placed the child in a box with a label saying "limited".

But what if we could train ourselves in the art of *open responses*? This would go along the lines of pausing and consciously quietening my mind; acknowledging the immediate, instinctive reaction; and then telling myself I need to find out more. A simple question to the child (not the adult) such as "Is this your first time swimming?" followed up maybe with a "What do you like doing?" To the parent I might then ask if there's anything for me to bear in mind to make the most of our time together in the water. From then on, the whole session becomes playfully exploring what we can do together, taking each discovery just that little bit further.

So the openness that helps me be at my best and enables the child to feel at ease, the two of us ready to try new things and have fun, starts with a *pause*. There is also an awareness and recognition of *preconceptions and judgements*. Openness in practice then shows itself in an *inquisitiveness or curiosity* – in part a disciplined, conscious commitment to find out more before settling on what might work in the session; in part an opening for connecting with, listening to and engaging with the person in front of me. What Stephen Rollnick would call "uncluttering the mind" in practice. Then the focus of the session, as suggested, can be all about *exploring possibilities* and, as we saw in the previous chapter, losing ourselves in the flow of our time together. And without being aware of it, the time flies by and we are left with a sense of quiet wonder at all that has been done.

Assured spaces

Our own early morning swim and the lesson with our young swimmer now done, we're back at the pool for the third and last time, ready to coach (leading or assisting) a typical evening club session. Amid all the commotion – of swimmers arriving, some buzzing, a few looking tired and disinterested; all the chatter and conversations; the need to check with the other coaches our plan for the evening (rarely done in enough time beforehand); set up equipment; always a few latecomers and at least two who forgot to pre-register – how do we find that inner self-confidence and stillness?

When I was fairly new to coaching, taking a busy, weekly club swim session on my own, I came to realize that, in one sense, it could actually be easier than I had initially thought. At the start, I was acutely aware of my relative inexperience and unsure of what I could bring. The noise and commotion all around made me feel out of place and hesitant as I struggled to hold on to what I had carefully planned to do in the coming session.

I realized, though, that there's a coaching space waiting to be filled and ready for me to step into. At a minimum the club members showing up for a swim expected someone to give them a session to get on with – I didn't need to force my way in, present my qualifications or check for their approval of what I had planned. And as it turned out pretty much all were accepting of how I changed the format of the sessions to a way that allowed me to feel in my element.

The idea of stepping into an expectant coaching space also offers us the chance to shape that space – how we, in effect, take command of it as ours and welcome those coming in, connect with them, make them feel safe, engaged and energized and ready to explore what is about to unfold. Think of an empty stage and a performing artist about to enter, ready to fill the awaiting space with their creative energy. For us as coaches it is hopefully not as nerve-racking but potentially even more sublime as we are not performing to a hushed, inert audience sitting afar in the dark. Together, athletes and coach are about to create an active, living experience full of our collective energy and possibilities, rich in attentive caring and opportunities for their and our own self-belief.

In those early days I hit on three Ps as a checklist to myself to help me feel more assured in shaping the way I wanted the sessions to run:

Purpose

Thinking through the specific purpose of each and every session, distilling it down into just a few words, visualizing how I would express this before I let the session start all helped.

Previously swimmers would drift in randomly, get straight in the water and do so many lengths' warm-up (always too fast) whilst the coach wrote up the set on a whiteboard, visible only to the top lanes. I changed things around, asking everyone to gather together before going in. I would quickly explain and demonstrate the particular technique we'd be focusing on, how it would help their swimming and the thinking behind the main part of the session. Not just having my own sense of the purpose but sharing this upfront seemed to energize and engage us all, giving a clear focus for each swimmer and a sense of sharing in a joint endeavour, clearly committed to their improvement.

Planning

Now, I'm not a natural methodical planner. So in those early sessions I would really labour over detailed plans, as I'd been taught to – so many lengths, metres, intensity of efforts calculated for each lane. The discipline of preparing detailed plans for each session certainly instilled in me a sense of being ready to give my best focus and attention. I'd write these out on large sheets for each lane, headlining the purpose and then the details of each set for the lane (the lower lanes covering less distance or less intensive efforts than the higher lanes).

Needless to say more often than not, adaptions needed to be made. And later on, when I coached much younger swimmers in other clubs, the plans typically needed to be more radically revised if not discarded in the moment. My planning became far more about *a clarity and simplicity of purpose*. And with that my own sense of an assured space grew, and in turn gave the swimmers the freedom and encouragement to stretch and enjoy themselves.

Projection

Initially, in the noisy, echoey swimming pool I thought this would all be about shouting loudly to be heard. And I remember going through my swim teacher qualifications and being told not to kneel down close to the swimmers but instead stand tall and PROJECT!

As Kate highlighted in the Reflective Conversation in the last chapter, how we find our individual voice is much more nuanced – about finding the ways to be heard that we are each comfortable with. I soon realized that my third P wasn't so much about voice projection as about how to express my *presence* – how I wanted to be and present myself in the space. At one level, the small details done well: dressed in a suitable top and shorts. More bravely, calling everyone close together and waiting silently for their attention. Expansive body language to amplify expression (there's a gesticulating Italian in me). Tone and pace – with lots of pauses to let the swimmers take in, reflect and respond. Most important of all, as we will see in the next chapter, being wholly present and attuned to those in front of me and to myself. And the shouty projection only ever needed very rarely, almost all the connections starting from a place of attentive listening.

And there again we have another paradox: that being heard starts with *listening* – to ourselves and to others.

But enough of swimming pools. In the next chapter we will move to dry land and focus on the development of trusting relationships between the coach and athlete, though the ripple effects mentioned above – from knowing and being true to ourselves and our values – will be a key theme. Before that, some reflections from another open and insightful Reflective Conversation.

Reflective Conversation: What we want and don't want to be with Tom Hartley, UK Coaching

Tom Hartley is a familiar face to many in the UK's coaching world as he regularly hosts webinars, online interviews and insightful discussions with other coaches. He has been responsible for coach development at UK Coaching and recently took on the role of Coaching Team Lead, overseeing the coaching team at UK Coaching and working closely with UK Sport and Sport England. He has some 25 years' experience in football coaching, both in the US and in the UK, in men's and women's football and across a range of age groups and levels. He was involved in the pioneering Football Association Skills Programme and in the last two years or so has worked with Oxford United's and Swindon Town's women's football clubs. He now leads Oxford's Emerging Talent Centre.

In an earlier conversation he described himself to me as something of a "feedback fanatic", big on reflecting on his own practice. So just the person to talk with, learn from and share ideas and experience about our own self-confidence and what "knowing and being the best coach we can be" means.

Beginnings

At the start of this chapter, it was suggested that we need to be wary of thinking the top coaches of professionals and elites are always the models for each of us to find ourselves at our best. Interestingly, Tom said in his early coaching days he had a clear sense of the kind of coach he *didn't* want to be: to not follow the coach-centric, autocratic models espoused at the time. Through his various qualification courses he believed that what was taken as the way to coach "doesn't have to be the way".

> "Authenticity is a word you hear a lot in coaching and… [the] language around 'being the best coach only you can be' resonates with me as I have spent a long time in coaching trying to find a way that feels like me, rather than copying others."

If you've seen Tom you'll know his quiet, considered demeanour is a long way from the stereotypical loud, big on instruction, not so great at listening model of coaching that you can imagine he was supposed to follow. In addition, Tom mentioned his own footballing didn't reach a level where he was directly influenced or overawed by top, professional coaches. For his part, he wanted to find a way of coaching that would be innovative, in tune with where the young players were at and true to himself.

As we talked, Tom's early story also made me wonder about the drive I have to coach and the coaching philosophy I've developed – *to always believe in the amazing things people can do with just the right degree of challenge, expert care and encouragement*. I came to running relatively late as a middle of the field also-ran, coming through to (albeit modest) prominence with the encouragement of a coach who saw something in me that, at the time, I didn't see in myself. Or maybe he was simply very generous. Looking back, although I respected them, I was less influenced by the more senior, expert and highly regarded coaches who seemed only to take an interest when I became more successful.

And in terms of our coaching journeys, Tom and I both seemed to have a stronger, sharper sense of what we didn't want to be before we found and felt comfortable with – let alone could put into words – the kind of coach we wanted to be. Although it may seem like dwelling on negatives, perhaps there's a place for some "don't want to be like…" models alongside identifying what we truly value, in the process distilling and articulating our philosophies.

Leaving the valley of humility with less is more

Tom also openly talked about his coaching journey following something of a pattern of the much-quoted Experience-Confidence Curve (in various versions drawn from Dunning-Kruger[24]).

Essentially, as applied in the coaching world, this captures the idea that we can start our coaching journeys in a burst of enthusiasm, high in confidence, sure of what we believe to be right. Then, with a little more experience, we realize our knowledge and expertise are actually far less than we'd assumed, and confidence drops. We might finally, and hopefully, steadily grow our expertise and a sense of the value we can bring. Tom talked about his own "valley of humility" – of a sense that the more experience he acquired, the less he felt he really knew and the more there was to learn.

Tom described his journey from this seemingly low, humbling point. In that earlier phase he tended to plan every coaching session down to the last detail: "I used to plan, plan, plan… and it never seemed enough." With greater experience he came to develop a more open, creative way of coaching – having a clear purpose and something of a plan, whilst allowing for the detail of how it unfolded to take care of itself. Tom cited Olympic canoe slalom coach Craig Morris, who we both admire: "be prepared rather than planned" – Tom adding in his words "Sometimes a little structure can allow a lot of freedom."

Later on in our conversation Tom referred to a session he'd coached earlier that week in which he wanted to encourage a more courageous, attacking play. Coming up with the ideas in the moment, rather than all pre-planned in detail, he progressively threw in a series of extra rules that disrupted how the players would normally have gone about an otherwise fairly conventional

---

[24] For the original: J. Kruger and D. Dunning 'Unskilled and unaware of it: how difficulties in recognizing one's incompetence lead to inflated self-assessments' in *Journal of Personality and Social Psychology*, 77 (6), 1121–1134 (1999).

practice. These included points deducted for any backward passes, much to the consternation of some of the players!

Resistance and dancing

Tom's example led us on to talk more generally about the resistance there can be when we do things differently and, in effect, shift the focus away from a coach's prescriptive instructions and instead to players and athletes working things out for themselves. "Just tell us what to do!" can be a typical response. I know some of the swimmers I have coached in a club session or squad are frustrated that I don't plainly tell them what to fix in their stroke, instead asking them what they are feeling, to experiment and experience for themselves what works.

And we noted how younger athletes can be so much more open to a playful, yet totally absorbing spirit of adventure, of having a go. I wonder whether this has something to do with high energy activity being its own reward, without the need for what looks "right" to a watching coach. If so, it suggests something very precious to nurture, rather than stifle with over-instruction. Knowing when to get out of the way, to keep quiet and let those we coach, young and old, learn from their own activity seems to me one of our biggest challenges in the art of genuinely athlete-centred, confidence-enriching coaching.

Tom went on to point out the delicate context for him – that some players will be concerned about being selected for the next game and wary of making mistakes or performing below what they feel is expected. In such an environment I imagine the coach must also be under pressure – to coach in a way that is expected, to fit into the culture and ways of working in the club. Tom talked about the uneasy dance between the players' needs and coach's expert knowledge, all performed under a spotlight of expectations, difficult-to-challenge assumptions and pressure to get results.

"I am aware that at times I might need to borrow some behaviours and coach in a way that sometimes feels uncomfortable because it might be right for the athletes at that moment in time… but playing to my strengths when coaching gives me confidence and helps me perform better and feel better about my impact as a coach."

Home

One final reflection from our conversation. Tom talked about his 10 years working at the Football Association's Skills Programme, designed for 5–11 year-old players across the UK. As he described it, the central aim was increased participation in football – rather than a selective spotting of future stars. This fitted perfectly with Tom's "kids first, then football" approach.

He also talked about the programme's learning environment and the strong focus on personal growth for coaches and coached. One aspect of this was a limit imposed on the number of hours of actual coaching to allow time for other sources of learning. Tom also spoke of role models who "showed us what great coaching could look like". Listening to Tom I had a sense of him having found a home for his way of coaching, the way he always wanted it to be. How brilliant.

And it made me reflect on how, in the likely absence of such a professional, highly developed set-up, with inspiring role models, we can create our own supportive "homes": always being stretched and learning whilst feeling valued and held; a sense of belonging without the need to pretend to be something we are not.

We will return to this theme in Chapter 9, on protecting our energy. For now, we move toward our next domain of confidence: the confidence and trust those we coach have in us.

Before we do, some final words from Tom, about our conversation:

> "I find conversations [like this] incredibly valuable as it helps me to think aloud and reflect on some of the experiences I have had along the years. Talking with someone about your own experiences can be a way of building your own self-awareness."

And some final ideas for the emerging landscape and to take into the next chapter:

• hold on to being the coach that feels true and right for you – it may take a while to get there (and you're sure to realize there isn't any end destination), but wow, will it be worth it!

- amidst all the noisy clamour and pressure to be seen to do what coaches are expected to do, there is a deeper knowing ourselves in the stillness: a calming, self-compassionate attentiveness to what really counts for each of us. To find our true voice we first have to listen to ourselves

- as in the previous chapter's discussion of the nature of confidence, we may not actually *feel* self-confidence, even as our experience and expertise grow. In this respect, the idea of climbing out of a "valley of humility" seems misplaced. The sense of how much more there is to learn is something precious to hold on to throughout our journeys

- never stop practising the art of openness: to the person in front of us and what they can do; to what can happen if we let go of trying to control and plan every detail; and the subtle, highly skilful, creative art of open, inquisitive responses.

4
Confidence in the coach

"People will forget what you said, people will forget what you did, but people will never forget how you made them feel."

Maya Angelou

AND SO WE turn from our own self-confidence as coaches to the confidence that those we coach have in us. Without them having some degree of belief in us and what we can do for them, how can we be effective in our coaching, let alone develop meaningful, impactful relationships of trust and respect?

In this chapter we will:

- look at trust-based coaching relationships, how they start, develop and grow, always holding the potential for something highly creative and rewarding for those we coach and for ourselves

- identify distinctive qualities of connection to make our own

- suggest some guiding principles and landmarks to help us navigate along what can be a rocky way, including when things take a wrong turn

- close with a Reflective Conversation, this one with someone outside of sports who brings deep insights into trust-based relationships.

Let's start with a fundamental principle. Trust is a highly personal, precious and in some respects precarious state to aspire to. It is not something to conjure up by applying top tips and tricks. Nor is it something that is owed, whatever the standing or experience of the coach or how well intentioned we are.

Our approach is different to that typically found in many coaching discussions, courses, webinars and online sound bites. Whilst useful as prompts to question ourselves or spur us on, these can have an element of an ideal confection, like recipes for baking the perfect cake. The key ingredients are identified to mix in the right conditions and there we have it – the perfect end product, ready to be admired and enjoyed. Many of the commonly cited ingredients – such as Professor Sophia Jowett's closeness, commitment, complementarity and co-orientation[25] – are indeed highly relevant and we are sure to include some of them along the way.

Yet our view will come from a different perspective, focusing on:

- key qualities of connection as the starting point of every relationship

- the different interests and needs of those we coach at different points in what can be a bumpy, uncertain path

- insights into openness, compassion and trust from possibly unusual, unexpected fields outside the word of sports coaching.

The qualities of connections on a cold October evening

Picture this: a young woman arrives for her first time at a track run session at the local triathlon club. We'll call her Hannah (not her real name). She has just started her first year at university, living away from home for the first time. Back there Hannah was a well-known, popular, much cared for rising star in her swim and run clubs, a junior cross-country champion and a regular in the school's netball team. Here she's pretty much a complete unknown in a very disorientating new world.

Wanting to find a place and others to train with, she did a Google search for "run clubs" in the city. There was a list of five, including a tri club that looked

---

[25] From a professorial acceptance speech at Loughborough University. Professor Jowett puts these first three Cs – a closeness as in mutual respect and liking for each other, a commitment to work together, working in a complementary style – as defining good quality relationships marked by, as she terms it, co-orientation around a shared purpose.

to be fun and friendly (at least the site looked that way) and might work for her swimming too. Would the time of sessions work for her? Where are they and how would she get there from her new student accommodation? And how open would they be to a young outsider? To students? To her?

She used the enquiries form on their site to ask if she could come along to the next run session without having to sign up to be a member. That same evening came a short, friendly reply saying she'd be welcome to come along on a "try us out" basis, and telling her it's £3 payable on the night ("Please bring the right change") and the name of the coach to pay.

She decided to give them a go, plucking up courage once again in a full-on month of new places, faces and situations. On the night, with a few wrong turns and locked gates, Hannah eventually found her way on to the track. There was a small group of men and women in Lycra leggings, some with matching club tops, all busy chatting in twos and threes, others clustered around an older guy wrapped in a warmer outfit.

Now, up until this point there have been just a few points of *contact* along the way – searching online, clicking through to a site, using a form and receiving an email reply. At each point an impression was made, a feeling left, doubts and uncertainties either allayed or deepened. All these and so much more from her first weeks at university are brought to the moment she steps forward at the track.

What happens next may, or may not, be a *connection*: a sense of being seen and held, first in that moment and then over the next hour; or, sadly, yet another distancing encounter that leaves her feeling isolated, disconnected, on her own and far from home. She may find the session itself hard or easy (Hannah actually ran the socks off the leading men, as we will see) – but it's the connections made that colour her experience of the evening, will leave her feeling that there is a place for her and make her keen to come again.

So what are the qualities of connections we as coaches can focus on in order for that to happen in such a momentary encounter? I think there are at least three that we can look to develop and nurture:

Being present

Perhaps it goes without saying but there is a real and direct sense in which we as coaches – in the words of Brené Brown – must "show up", bringing ourselves to each encounter, each session and interaction with those we coach. In *On Connection*, Kae Tempest talks about how too often we are merely "maintaining a surface level engagement with whatever is going on while at the same time being entirely elsewhere".

If I am too preoccupied with all the "elsewhere" clutter in my head, I'm likely to come to the session with a weary, going through the motions attitude. Not much chance of turning points of contact into moments of connection. Here we go back to the unhurried composure, attentive focus on the person in front of us, the finding and losing ourselves at our very best that we saw in the chapter on the nature of confidence. I have to be "absolutely located" in the here and now to connect with the shy, young newcomer in front of me as well as with each of the other regular runners.

> "Connection is the feeling of landing in the present tense. Fully immersed in whatever occupies you, paying close attention to the details of experience. Characterised by an awareness of your minuteness in the scheme of things. A feeling of being absolutely located. Right here. Regardless of whether that 'right here' is agitated or calm, joyous or painful."
>
> Kae Tempest, *On Connection*[26]

Magical mastery of time

There is another critical quality of the connection to be made and this has a certain magic about it. So often when we are under pressure at the start of a session – with a stream of people arriving, a prepared plan to get through, equipment to sort out – we can be caught up in a busy rush. We then go away at the end feeling dissatisfied that there just wasn't time for everything. Yet by slowing ourselves down just long enough to be attentive to others and to ourselves, even for just a few seconds or minutes, time seems to expand. The hour seems to be more than adequately filled and afterwards we wonder at how so much has been done.

And for those we connect with there can be a similar concertina effect of stretching out and compressing time. What might actually amount to only

---

[26] K. Tempest *On Connection* (2020).

one or two, maybe three minutes of attentiveness – an unrushed interest shown at the start, a few encouraging words along the way, a moment at the end to ask how it was and a "hope we see you next week" – may feel to them much longer and be a defining memory of the evening. By the same token, a momentary inattentiveness whilst we're distracted by other things or just not focused can mark their experience of the whole session, dragged out over what will seem longer than an hour.

One of the most valuable practical guides I picked up in this respect is called the *10 and 2 rule*. I wish I knew the name of the tutor on an Active Sussex coaches' workshop many years ago who shared this as it has been such a helpful guide to me. The tutor – all credit to him, whoever he was – said that when someone comes to our sessions we have just 10 seconds to make them feel welcome. Ten seconds. If we miss that brief window an impression is set and we will always be making up the lost opportunity. And the two is that we then have around two minutes to set the tone of the session to come.

Ten seconds. To look someone in the eye, smile and say "welcome", to introduce ourselves, ask their name and find out more about them. Or, if we know them already, to greet them by name, say "great to see you", maybe ask how they are or what they've been doing. In both cases, we are showing an attentive interest and readiness to engage and connect. All quite simple and obvious but so easily skated over.

And just as an aside, I remember to my embarrassment, taking my two minutes to explain to newcomer Hannah the structure of the track session and suggest she focus on her own pace. "Don't worry about the faster lead men who'll be racing each other way off at the front." No sooner did the hard intervals start, two men breaking away from the rest, than I could see a look of consternation on their faces as she tucked in behind them, kept pace, started to push them harder than they were used to and then moved ahead! A good lesson for me about not making assumptions.

Shared purpose

Our final critical quality of connection in coaching is a single-minded, meaning-filled intent: a genuine interest and commitment to helping those in front of us in whatever endeavour they may have. Our connections have an underlying, consistent intention – to find and bring out the best in those we coach and in ourselves. It may seem obvious, but how easy it is to lose our way in all the details of the act of coaching – the *doing* of coaching rather than the *why* as in the attentive, intentional *being* a coach.

And here lies another key principle of confidence-centred coaching: to treat the ambitions of the person in front of us as a precious gift we are privileged to share in. As we will see, this comes into its own in longer-term coaching. On the night at our track session, our connection with a whole group of runners to be made in just an hour or so, showing a simple interest can have such a strong, meaning-filled impact. Perhaps a brief "How's it going with your training?" to show ourselves as alongside and interested in our runners' progress. Holding in mind that each of them will have had their own journeys to get there and each brings with them their hopes and doubts.

Worth pausing a moment to notice that in such an open, curious questioning we want to avoid sparking any hint of judgement or conditions for our interest as coaches. I hear of so many clubs where on arrival a newcomer is immediately quizzed about their ability, their personal best times or how much training they do, as if they must be at a certain level to be worthy of further attention. I wonder, had I asked Hannah about her PBs what would have happened. No doubt I would have been super impressed and excited at the prospect of a bright new talent joining us. And I definitely wouldn't have bothered with the well-intentioned but totally misplaced advice about ignoring fast men at the front! Yet would that have made her feel any more welcomed, held in the moment and valued for herself rather than her times?

It doesn't take much sensitivity to realize that, above all, our young newcomer on this cold October evening is looking to find a friendly place to run free and feel great in herself whilst making her place in a very new, at times overwhelming world.

How brilliant if we can train ourselves to bring an open inquisitiveness, a deft mastery of time and a deep regard and respect for the ambitions of the people in front of us to those first points of contact and thereby create a meaningful connection. From there lies the prospect of beginning to develop a trusting, rewarding relationship that we now turn to.

Principles and landmarks along an uncertain path

Let's go back for a moment to our image of the perfectly confected trust cake. And here's the thing. As a coach I may have a clear idea of the ingredients that will make for the ideal trusting relationship. But can I expect these to be shared right from the outset by those in front of me? The members of a team, a squad or someone coming for individual coaching support? Their journeys are certain to be very different to mine, even if at some point we align and travel side by side.

Charles Feltman, renowned authority on trust in the workplace, has an insightful definition of trust (quoted below). I am drawn first to the element of *choice*. I see this as a tentative, finding our way to what feels right, rather than a rational weighing up of conscious choice. And interestingly he also highlights the riskiness, vulnerability, the *letting go* that has been a theme throughout our exploration of confidence-centred coaching.

"trust is defined as choosing to risk making something you value vulnerable to another's actions."

Charles Feltman[27]

So how can we find our way through this potential mismatch of motives and a changeable landscape? A model I first came across when working on supplier relationships in the business world (I've had a very wide-ranging career) has helped me orientate myself through developing relationships with some of the athletes I coach. There is nothing that says one stage must inevitably lead on to the next – nor can anything be gained by trying to require a coached athlete to shift from one stage to another. It's a journey that we can be alongside but not hurry or force along.

Calculative scepticism

Here's what can typically happen. An athlete may have heard from others that I coach their particular sport. They might have seen on the website a brief outline of how I work, the kind of clients I've worked with in the past, stories of their challenges, the fees involved.

We meet and quickly try to get a feel for whether we will work together. It's all a bit hesitant and tentative as if exploring how comfortable we each feel before jumping to a commitment. At that point and in all likelihood

---

[27] From C. Feltman *The Thin Book of Trust: An essential primer for building trust at work* (2021).

for some time after, for the athlete there can be something of an uneasy calculation forming in their mind – "Will this coach really be able to help me with my goal? To give me an extra edge? Will the fee be worth it?" A big "cost" being weighed up, consciously or unconsciously, is certain to be what changes to their current training and lifestyle they might be asked to make.

Needless to say, we cannot expect a prospective or new client to immediately trust us when they are weighing everything up, unsure and yet to be convinced of the worth of the relationship. Making bold promises about guaranteed results, if anything, may generate a veneer of excitement yet prompt a deeper underlying wary scepticism.

From my experience I sense the following can help:

- patiently accepting that the athlete needs to work through these calculations for themselves without pressure

- being upfront about what is likely to be involved, what the coaching support consists of, painting the picture of how we will work and seeking to allay fears of hidden "costs"

- above all, showing our genuine interest, belief and respect for their ambitions.

Hopefully we begin to see a shift away from an uneasy calculation of costs and benefits toward a recognition that they have met someone ready to be alongside in realizing their goals.

Hesitant trial

Trust is slowly earned. Even when the calculations have been worked through, many will need to prove to themselves that the training I might be suggesting really does help – particularly if it is different to what they have done before. This is such a key step: being willing to give something a try and being open to what will happen.

Whilst a new client might appear excited and apparently "up for it", I have found this can sometimes mask an uncertain, hesitant attitude to giving a new approach a try. Only later might they admit to such ambivalence and hesitancy.

I recall one client honestly sharing something of her uncertain path through this uneasy terrain of *calculative scepticism* and *hesitant trial*. Initially Gill tried to keep going with the way she had always trained and somehow add in what I had recommended, despite an obvious clash between her big on volume and intensity way of training and my attention to recovery and a less is more approach. Close to exhaustion and dispirited, at her husband's insistence she eventually gave my suggestions a chance. She soon felt the benefits, revealingly writing in a later post "1–0" to me the coach (not that I was keeping score). Gill stuck, more or less, to the new approach, gradually willing to try very different sessions and more recovery. Trust as "making something you value vulnerable to another's actions" (with a record-breaking first place to boot).

Perhaps some of those we coach have to reach a point of despairing that nothing is working in order to make that step to an almost reluctant trial – "What else have I got to lose?" steps into "Might as well give it a try. Let's see what happens."

What will help us and our athletes in this rocky terrain? Insisting on "Do what I say," "my way or the highway" is very unlikely to work, as it would merely entrench their reluctance and heighten a feeling that it is all or nothing, with no recognition of their uneasy ambivalence. In contrast, we may have more success by:

- looking to understand what lies behind their unease in letting go of a previous way of training, rather than summarily dismissing what they have done (even if we both can see it led to injury or burnout)

- explaining the purpose and thinking behind every plan, phase and prescribed session

- being patient even when we see our suggestions not fully followed through, ready to understand the hesitancy

- emphasizing that we are engaged in a joint endeavour to find what works, that it will be different for each athlete and we don't always have all the answers

- knowing in ourselves that what we suggest comes from a place of wanting them to find themselves at their very best.

Bond of trust

The ideal point in our journey – where we want to get to – is an easy bond of trust. The scepticism and doubting are unlikely ever to entirely go, but they take much more of an inquisitive, explorative form. The athlete's focus turns from questioning our ability as a coach to more of a shared quest to learn together and see what can be achieved.

What does this look and feel like? First is a sense of *easy mutual respect*. I hope to get to a place where there is a comfortableness with those I coach – not coach-can-do-no-wrong, on a pedestal; but a more balanced and discerning sense of them knowing what they value and how what I bring complements their individual needs. A relationship between two human beings, each with our own histories, strengths and vulnerabilities. Leave the hard work of infallibility to the Pope and any excessive reverence at the door. They'll just get in the way of a trusting, open, mutually respectful way of working together.

Second is what might be thought of as *clarity of commitment with and without words*. Explicitly setting out the terms of course has its place, particularly as we saw at the start of the relationship. Yet it is without the words where the trusting relationship comes alive. As we get into the routine of weekly coaching calls, regular reviews and the build-up to and then coming down from big events, the need to fall back on a formal commitment seems to fade away. We quickly get to a point of knowing implicitly that each is committed to making the coaching relationship work.

A third feature of the state of trust that I hope to arrive at and keep tending to is an *in reflection generosity*. I recall how, in my earlier days of starting to coach athletes privately one-to-one, I could be thrown into doubt at even small hiccups along the way. An athlete hadn't recorded whether they completed a prescribed session that we had talked through in advance – "Maybe they've given up on being coached? What did I do wrong? Didn't I make it clear enough?" Or maybe they missed a scheduled coaching call and I'm plunged into questioning the whole set-up – "Should I chase them up? What about other coaches and how they work? Maybe I should change the way I work… though to what?"

Learning to be more generous to myself took a while – to not react to the messiness of real-life coaching as if everything were a judgement on my competence. There's a generous trusting in ourselves and how we coach that I want to nurture – captured nicely for us in the Reflective Conversation with Kate Offord at the end of Chapter 2.

And our assumption of generosity extends to those we coach – not taking those missed calls, no-shows at training or gaps in the training log as a sign that they have not committed and bought in to what we want to achieve together. Here, once more, is the power of that small word "yet" that Carol Dweck talks about – "I don't understand why they missed that session after all we'd agreed… yet. So I'd better find out before jumping to conclusions."

What happens from there on is where the coaching relationship comes alive: the sense of exploring together the outer limits of what can be achieved; an openness to learning all the time; as we will see in Chapter 6, the creativity and inventiveness in the moment that can happen seemingly out of nowhere to surprise us.

When things go wrong

It doesn't always work so well, though, does it? Even with the biggest dose of reflective generosity and our very best intentions, we can find ourselves struggling to make a meaningful connection, let alone arrive at an easy, trusting, mutually respectful relationship.

Let's take three all too typical examples that regularly feature in peer groups I belong to. First, despite our best efforts to connect with young people in our sessions, we may come up against what feels like a determined wall of disengagement. No matter how patient, listening and ready to go with their suggestions, we can't seem to get through. Or a second typical case: we find that an athlete we have started working with just doesn't follow through on what we thought had been painstakingly discussed, settled on and understood – typically doing a session much harder or for longer than had been talked through at length and agreed (or so we thought). And our third dispiriting common example: a relationship we assumed was going well is ended abruptly without warning or explanation, in some cases the athlete switching to another coach. The jump typically is to a coach who had a more dazzling athletic career in their younger days – as if this somehow makes them any more successful (and trustworthy) as a coach.

Answers? Questions!

Our minds are instantly full of seemingly unanswerable questions: "How on earth can I get through?!" "Why don't they just do what we agreed?!" "How could they – after all I've done?!"

I say seemingly unanswerable but in fact our reactions suggest we are already putting together a stock of ready-made answers.

We might tell ourselves the disengaged teenagers have (as if by definition) "issues" which they will eventually grow out of, preferably without our involvement. Rather than look for connection we end up retreating to some form of low expectation, manageable containment. The frustratingly errant, mind of their own athlete can be shrugged off with a dry, stoical (if truth be told smug) "They'll learn the hard way." Maybe laughed off as a "hopeless case" – or even worse, in our minds dismissed as "un-coachable". And the magpies who alight on the next shiny thing they see were always just that – fickle and unappreciative of the real value we bring. Or so we might tell ourselves.

Yet this is the thing: in the absence of really knowing what is going on for any one of these typical cases we are likely to jump to ready-made, limiting stories and assumptions about them.

Questions? Answers!

And so we go back to the distinction made in the previous chapter, between *closed reactions* and *open responses*. Our initial reactions can, in effect, be a closing down: a dismissive labelling of those in front of us that limits both them and us. Yet as was suggested, we can train ourselves in the art of skilful openness: a stilling pause to see our initial reaction as not a definitive answer but the prompt to find out more, to ask ourselves and those in front of us the simplest and most open of questions. Always adding a "What else?"

Here we'll take a quick dive into a very different pool of knowledge and insight. Writers on looking at art have given me valuable lessons that help deepen the skills of open responses[28]. Imagine standing before a big, bold piece of abstract modern art. Or maybe a 17th-century portrait of some noble family in all their old-world finery. Our initial reaction might be a disdainful "Doesn't do anything for me!"

---

[28] The School of Life *Art Against Despair* (2022) provides thoughtful insights and perspectives on what we can learn and reflect on from an extraordinarily wide range of art. See also M. Findlay, *Seeing Slowly: Looking at Modern Art* (2017).

In *Art as Therapy*[29], Alain de Botton and John Armstrong suggest that the first and most crucial step to overcoming what they call our "defensiveness" – a rush to distance ourselves from any engagement – is "to be generously aware of how normal it is to harbour strongly negative views about things". Their second step involves a recognition of how alien and different the artists' worlds are certain to have been to our own. And if we choose, with that comes a readiness to find out more: what was the context? What might their world have been like? What might they have wanted to express? And how might it have been received? The third step is then to look for points of connection to which we can relate our own experiences and feelings.

And back to the coaching, it is in looking for empathetic connections to our own experiences that we might find some answers to those frustrating instances when the relationships feel strained or maybe aren't happening at all. How different might my reactions be toward the resolutely disengaged young person if I can think back and reconnect to my own teenage years? The listless confusion of not wanting to be wherever it was I happened to be, but not knowing where I wanted to be instead; wanting to be listened to but not knowing what I wanted to say or how to put my feelings into words; wanting to be seen for who I was but unsure what that might be and fearing I might stand out as different.

And thinking of the athlete who keeps doing more than I thought we had painstakingly agreed, I might recall how anxious I can still feel facing a big challenge, beyond anything I'd trained for before. "Less is more? You must be joking!" "Do more easy sessions and make them easier? When I know how hard it's going to be?" If I can tap into these feelings, our conversations are sure to be coloured by a more compassionate care, a readiness to listen and understand – even when suggesting an approach initially at odds with the athlete's desire to be doing their own thing.

Hardest of all, perhaps, is when we have put the best of ourselves out there, invested time and effort in making a relationship work – and find it is apparently disregarded. The magpie has flown. The easy mutual respect has been one-way. The commitment all one-sided. Our generosity taken for granted. And of course some endings are very ragged, magpies not being known for their thoughtfulness or graciousness.

---

[29] A. de Botton and J. Armstrong *Art as Therapy* (2013).

Self-compassion and not retaliating

Talking with other coaches, sharing similar stories, my sense is that we can brood for a time with the frustration, exasperated and unable to make much sense of what has happened, then all too quickly tell ourselves to move on – like sticking with our first, defensive, disregarding reaction to a painting in a gallery before hurrying along to something we feel more comfortable with. Perhaps we are affected by an unsettling self-doubt, of not having done a good enough job, of not being a good enough coach. Best not to dwell on it.

Yet we can take the same steps we took to understand those we coach and, in that way, understand ourselves and our feelings. We might start with a self-compassionate, generous acknowledgement of the rawness of the feeling. Just sitting with it rather than rushing on. We can reflect on our own context, asking ourselves what it is in our make-up that someone has (inadvertently) hooked in to and triggered a strong reaction. Then we can start to reconnect to the very best of ourselves – to remind ourselves of the reasons why we coach and the fact that sometimes being upset by others' actions comes from a place of caring deeply about doing the best we can.

What we can't do is retaliate. Sometimes the height of great coaching might be calmly holding back, staying silent yet present, true to ourselves and what we believe, no matter the provocation. And here's the thing. If coaching at its very best was only about high performance, about transferring our expertise to help a willing athlete to amazing results, then we might take a "win some, lose some" attitude – focusing our efforts on those who respond to our efforts. Yet what if we saw the heights of leading edge coaching at its very best, at its most skilful, challenging and rewarding, as being alongside the unresponsive, angry or anxious? To listen to the unheard? Connect with the hard to engage? And show a belief and readiness to trust in those who have little belief in themselves and others?

In this respect the recipes for perfectly confected models of coaching that we mentioned at the start of the chapter are interesting but don't capture the reality and richness of creating meaningful, impactful, trusting relationships. And although there are some great, inspiring examples of leading, high-profile coaches to learn from, we may do better by seeking out those at the edge of extraordinary practice in other fields: those who are skilled in the art of developing deep, impactful, restorative relationships; empathic listening; and compassion in action.

Reflective Conversation: What happens in the room with Margo Bristow

Which is why our next Reflective Conversation goes outside the world of sports coaching to that of psychotherapy. The following reflects on an insightful conversation with Psychotherapist Margo Bristow from Illinois, USA. Margo specializes in what she described to me as "harm reduction in young people": young people who come to her with a wide range of addictive, damaging behaviours, such as substance abuse, or compulsive behaviours, such as gambling and shoplifting.

I first came across Margo through MI webinars, hosted by Stephen Rollnick and Joel Porter. Margo regularly contributes to the discussions of empathy in action, restorative practices and other themes. She brings a sense of deep compassion, patience and belief in the capacity of the young people she works with to live fulfilling lives. Who better to help us explore themes of connection and trust in the most demanding and challenging relationships?

On entering the room

I wanted, first, to explore with her what happens when a young person enters her consulting room for the first time – in all likelihood carrying a lot of anger, confusion or hurt. How can a relationship of trust begin so that the young person is able to open up, to be at their most vulnerable and to give voice to their most raw and troubling emotions? And for this to happen without her, as the therapist, revealing much of herself at all?

Of course those who step into a therapist's room are there because they have reached a point where there is some sense of needing help beyond what they can summon up in themselves – though in our conversation Margo said some of those she sees are there reluctantly by order of a court or through pressure from family members. She meets each with a kindly, unpressured "Since you have to be here, how can we work together?" From there, whether enforced or by free choice, it was clear Margo's work is imbued with a sense of holding each and every young person with the utmost care, patience and respect.

"Putting self aside"

Key to this seemed to be what Margo described as "putting self aside". I sensed this had several elements, starting with a finely tuned vigilance about her own emotions and reactions. She might find herself so moved by a young person that she wants to reach out to them, hug them and in some way – any way – make things better. Yet even the most heartfelt, compassionate urge can come from a place of the therapist themselves wanting to feel better, as if unable to contain their own emotions. But for the healing to work, Margo explained, she must hold herself in check and focus on making the space for the client to find their own clarity (as she termed it).

The same resolve to be so deeply and purposively client-centred was evident when Margo talked about instances of young people who come with extremist, obnoxious views of the world. I was struck by the experiences and insights she shared. One of these was about a 15-year-old boy, in a rage with the world, full of racist, antisemitic and other hate-fuelled views. Margo revealed that in such moments she might ask herself "Will another therapist be able to help better?"

From our conversation, I sensed this was not egoistic, not comparing herself to others; nor looking for an easy way out – another therapist to pass the problem child on to. The sense I got was of her questioning herself to bring forward the very best qualities in her practice – the patient attentiveness and commitment to a tender search for the young person's own clarity and sense of self-worth. Not in the same league, I know, but Margo made me think of the composure and clear-sightedness I would want to bring when faced with a particularly challenging athlete – "Could another coach do better?" might lead me to look more carefully at what will be needed from me at my very best.

She went on to outline the traumas, the neglect and the judgemental and disempowering environment her young, angry client had experienced in his upbringing. As she spoke, I felt my own instinctive disdain for the person she described and their obnoxious views shift to sorrow for him and anger toward those who disregarded him at such an impressionable, vulnerable age. Needless to say, it didn't make me feel any softer about hate-filled speech and action, but I could feel the range of my own emotional response broaden.

This led us on to Margo talking about the difficult challenge of remaining true to her own beliefs and values – as in the case above – when they are totally at odds with those stridently espoused by the client in the room. Again that resolute discipline of "putting self aside" came through. It is as if being authentic and true to herself is precisely shown in not responding with counter-arguments or rebukes, but in holding the space for him to vent his anger and alienation and from there together explore more deeply where those feelings come from and where he wants to go.

Belief and wisdom in the room

I was also struck and moved by Margo's absolute belief in the strength and wisdom of the young people she works with. It came through at several points in our conversation.

Margo talked about how therapists, especially when starting out, can be worried about whether they will be good enough or effective. In contrast, she disarmingly affirmed "The client will give us all that we need" – said with such a contented smile, clearly founded on years of her faith in those who come to see her being rewarded. Incidentally, the rage-filled boy returned some years later as a young man on the threshold of a new career and said "I think I may owe you an apology," realizing how personally offensive some of his hate-filled talk would have been to Margo.

Later on I asked her about an expression I've heard her use in the MI webinars: "The wisdom is in the room." Here is a fundamental belief in the client knowing themselves and what will work for them. As an example, she recounted her work with a small therapy group of young people convicted of shoplifting: "They tell me the triggers and what is effective... I need to go to that wisdom. I am constantly listening out for the wise person in the 13 year old... My wisdom is only to reflect on what they've said."

Just pause a moment to take that in! What extraordinary, compassionate belief in others and highly attuned listening. Isn't that a skill you would want to bring to each and every coaching relationship?

It's not about me

One final thought to mention from our conversation that made me reflect on those I coach. It goes back to what Margo said about getting out of the way and "putting self aside". I asked her about the imbalance between patient and therapist: one being so open about their innermost self, the other setting clear boundaries around what they reveal of themselves. My own therapist put this nicely to me: that I only know her from what happens in the room. Margo explained that, particularly in her work with young people and families, if she shared even the barest of information about her own home life, the client would inevitably be drawn into making comparisons, embellished with all sorts of imagined assumptions. And the focus would shift away from the patient finding their own clarity.

This made me aware of how easy it can be to fall into recounting my own experience at a particular event an athlete is preparing for, without really knowing what they might take from the conversation: "When I did that race…" "When I went to the World Championships…" But do I really need to prove myself as a coach by laying claim to past achievements? And could I inadvertently be adding to the pressure they already feel? Or implanting a notion of what will count as success that has more to do with my past accomplishments than the rich, personal meaningfulness of what lies ahead for them?

In Margo's words toward the end of our conversation "Keep your own *mishigas* out of the room!"

So some of the key features we want to make a part of our new world of coaching, as we move on to coaching for confidence, include:

- the long-lasting effect of connections made in the moment, requiring us to be fully present, masters of time, clear and consistent in our purpose – and able to connect to our own experiences without making them the central focus

- the wonder and artistry of relationships of easy, high mutual respect, rooted in a trusting inquisitiveness about what can be discovered together

- a calming acceptance of what we might not easily understand and a readiness to look more deeply

- listening with compassion and belief as a core skill to work on continuously and practise in every encounter.

5
Coaching for confidence

"It's hard to put into words – but so clear, like a before and after switch."

Kat Ganly

S o FAR WE'VE explored and opened up the idea of confidence, looking more deeply at the underlying experience of what is actually *felt*. We have delved into our own *self-confidence as coaches*. And we have mapped out the journeys those we coach can take in developing *trusting relationships and confidence in us*. Now we turn to how we can *coach for confidence*: how to help those we coach experience for themselves and be changed by the underpinning feeling, so they are excited and ready to find their best in whatever challenges lie ahead.

And as I write this I'm wondering if some coaches have looked at the contents page and jumped straight to this chapter, looking for the what-to-do fixes and solutions, the top tips to put into practice? If so, a warm "Hi there" and "Welcome." This chapter certainly has a strong practical focus, yet not of a one size fits all nature.

We will:

• set out the briefest of recaps and some initial pointers for our coaching for confidence

- go for a run in the company of an extraordinary ultra distance athlete as she relives for us her experience of what she called her "confidence switch"

- introduce our Four Ps of Confidence-Centred Coaching: a model framework for working with an athlete on whatever their challenge may be

- further open up our understanding of what it is to truly feel and know a confidence shift in another Reflective Conversation.

Recap

Our approach is rooted in:

- understanding what confidence *feels* like, and seeking out and nurturing those feelings in both our own coaching and for those we coach

- *knowing and being true to ourselves* and our values as the starting point for creating *assured spaces* that bring out the best in us and those we coach

- *a deep respect for people's ambitions and aspirations* and an inquisitiveness about their *uniqueness* that allows us to connect and sets us on an albeit sometimes rocky, uncertain path of trust.

In Chapter 2: Rethinking confidence we suggested that there is something of a paradox about confidence: we can be acutely aware of its absence, but not so its presence. Instead, we want to seek out and nurture a mix of liberating, enabling, underpinning emotions and feelings:

- an *excitement*, experienced as a thrilled anticipation about what may lie ahead

- a sense of *control* and, at the same time, an easiness with those things we can't control, experienced as a stilling calmness and composure

- a *fluency* in the moment, experienced as mind and body in sync and what is often referred to as flow.

So our challenge is not so much about "building confidence" in an athlete, a phrase often used with great conviction but little sense of how or what is really happening. Instead, the challenge is to help those we coach seek out and nurture the underpinning feelings.

How might this be done? A few pointers before we get into more detail:

Coaching for excitement

The ideas here are very much in tune with some of the new thinking around what defines success[30]. Is success end results measured in wins or losses, times or podium places? Or is it about bringing everything together on the day, all that training and planning, finishing with a sense of having found ourselves at our very best? Beyond results achieved, what is going to make the event an amazing, memorable experience? What else? And if we help those we coach be in touch with the deeper significance of their challenge, we can together cultivate an enriching sense of shared purpose and excitement.

Coaching for control

As we suggested, control is more than meticulous preparation – critical though that it is. Nor is it an obsessive buttoning down of every detail that might impact on the day, notwithstanding the benefit of all those marginal gains. We want those we coach to find a calming sense of composure, being as ready as they can be whilst also having an easy acceptance of the things that can't be controlled. There is no better signal than the example we set day, to day, the behaviours we model when things go wrong (as they will) or the unexpected inevitably happens. The coach as a model of staying true to a deeper perspective and clear vision.

Coaching for fluency

And can we coach for that magical mind and body in sync state of flow? I believe so. It starts with a consistent focus on helping athletes develop their own relaxed alertness (to borrow a phrase from Psychologist Eric Fromm) to their *form*, *effort* and *movement*. Perhaps these come more naturally in the sports I coach – though they are largely absent from how we are taught to coach. *Form* is a composed attentiveness to how we hold ourselves and what we feel in our bodies in the water, on the bike or as we run. *Effort* is all about being able to read and control energy, to know instinctively how hard to push, sensing what levels can be sustained without tipping over into fatigue, without relying on a fancy gadget. And *movement* is about being attuned to a

---

[30] Two great examples are C. Bishop *The Long Win* (2024) and P. Grange *Fear Less* (2020).

rhythm and balance through each swim stroke, pedal turn or stride. Talking with coaches from other sports suggests such a focus on form, effort and fluency has just as much relevance beyond swim, bike and run – with the added dimension in team sports of a "relaxed alertness" to others.

Imagine how different it would be to coach this way, rather than the conventional focus on instructional technique and tactics, the coach owning "the right way" and success measured narrowly as end results. Genuinely athlete-centred coaching in a very different landscape, marked by a skilled attuning of ourselves to what is felt, by us and by those we coach; a deep regard for their uniqueness and an inquisitiveness to find out the limits of what is possible, then go beyond them.

Truly knowing over hundreds of miles

For now though it's time to go out for a run – though not just any run. We are in the company of a close friend and ultra distance runner Dr Kat Ganly as she recounts what she called a big "confidence switch". We will journey through places where confidence is *truly known and felt* and theory comes alive. We're in for a long run – hang in there as it'll be revealing.

First, a little background: some years ago I ran short sections alongside Kat on a series of daunting 100-mile events. At our tri club she shyly let it be known she had just completed a 100-mile run along the Thames and had three more to do in the year as part of a Centurion Running Grand Slam Challenge – would anyone possibly mind accompanying her on sections of the next 100-miler, across the South Downs? A team quickly took shape and over the remaining three epic runs we took it in turns relay style to run with her through the nights. It was quite an experience and influenced many of the ideas and practices in this book. We'll pick up more lessons from some of her other epic runs in the chapter on resilience.

For now, it's her experience of what she described as a switch in her confidence – a distinctive before and after – that she recounts for us as we run. Her story has two impactful discoveries along the way.

The fear and its undoing

Kat had already completed an Ironman triathlon, a gruelling SwimRun event and several ultra runs – including the legendary six-day Marathon des Sables in the Sahara Desert. So an experienced ultra athlete by any measure. As she explains it, though, when she ran in those big events it was with a fear of not making it to the end. The idea of not finishing, a DNF, was "the worst thing ever". Talking through some of her earlier big events, Kat recounts a sense of always having to hold back in case she overdid it and wouldn't be able to finish – running with a guilty, burdensome feeling of not wanting to let down those who had come out to support her along the way.

Two DNFs began a shift in this way of thinking. First she attempted the notorious Dragon's Back. This is classed as the toughest multi-day mountain race in the world: around 380km with 17,000 metres of ascents, running down the spine of Wales from North to South on mainly trackless, remote and at times severely scary mountainous terrain. Sure enough, this proved to be extremely tough. Kat says she felt "so far out of my depth" and not at all embarrassed about dropping out on the second day, having given it a "good go".

A second DNF came soon after in the 100-mile Arc of Attrition, round the coast of Cornwall. The weather was atrocious and the terrain unrelenting. Kat got to around 60 miles and realized she really wasn't interested in carrying on to the end. She continued on to the last aid station, only 15 miles from the end, and although she could have carried on, decided she wasn't bothered about finishing She felt relaxed about dropping out at that point. "I just wasn't interested." And with that came a realization: "I stopped – and nothing terrible happened!"

Fluency

Next up: Kat's extraordinary performances in the four Centurion Grand Slams gained her a place in an invitation-only Grand Union Canal ultra: Britain's longest non-stop ultra marathon at 145 miles, from Birmingham to London. She describes this – still with a tinge of surprise in her voice – as the best race of her life.

It didn't start so well, though. Going into the event she felt unprepared, never having run beyond 100 miles non-stop and unsure how to train for the extra distance. She also had a heel injury that limited how much she could do. Travelling up she felt pretty glum, stayed in a noisy hotel and woke up after only around three hours' sleep, in tears and convinced she couldn't do it. She brought to mind other runners with comparable performances to her own who had completed it, as if to try to convince herself it could be done, against everything she was feeling. Her partner gave a calming "We're here now so why not give it a go?" and reluctantly she went to the start.

So, with the most unpromising preparation and state of mind, she started – and as the miles passed gradually began to feel better. Having begun tearful, tired and with no expectation to finish, she found herself warming up and feeling stronger. She passed through the marathon distance in a new PB and at 50 miles was the first-placed woman. "I was still feeling grumpy – but wasn't feeling worse." At that stage there was also an element of not wanting to waste her partner's time and others' in her support team.

Having started "feeling so crap", as she concisely puts it, her habitual mindset of holding back for fear of what might come just wasn't there. Why hold back when she already felt bad and had little expectation of finishing? And somehow, through running in this more uninhibited state, without fearing the worst, various positives started to excite her. When planning for the event she had assumed that by around 50 miles it would be getting dark, but 50 miles came and went and it was still light. At the 70-mile mark the aid station was just being set up and night only beginning to fall. She had anticipated this would have been the hardest point, with under half the distance done and a whole night of running ahead – but instead she felt like she didn't want to stop. She kept the pace going and notched up another PB: for 100 miles. Four hours faster than her previous best!

"I don't know what happened after that." Up to around 120 miles she says she was all right, then "things started to hurt" (which I think we can safely take as a massive understatement). We will come back to Kat being in a place of pain in Chapter 8 on resilience. For now, picture her at the finish line: utterly exhausted, elated, the best run of her life.

Soon after came another invitation-only event: a new 62-mile off-road London to Brighton run being trialled for the first time. With the experience of the Grand Union Canal, she found herself able once again to run faster than she had ever done before. She recalls the sense of being okay to push herself to the limit, knowing that she could pull back if needed and the consequences wouldn't be dropping out – not that it would be such a bad thing if it happened anyway. "It might seem obvious" – and Kat says it would have been something she would have freely accepted on an intellectual level – but for the first time she could "truly feel and know it".

The confidence switch and what it is to truly know

So what do we see in Kat's switch in confidence? Well, there is that sense of *excitement* – of entering a space where we are surprised by what we can do, as opposed to the unnerving feeling of hoping for the best and waiting for the worst. Kat went from running holding the fear of not finishing, and expecting that to be her fate, to running with a lighter sense of seeing where it took her. And it's worth saying, with that seemed to come a change in how she felt about the support of those close to her. "I didn't want to let anyone down but it was not like before – I now wanted to make people feel proud and excited."

We can also see something of a sense of calm, composed *control*. Kat says it was a revelation to realize she could push herself, that she would be sufficiently in tune with her body to know when to ease back so she needn't hold back for fear of any failure nor impending pain. "If it gets too much I can just back off a bit." She accepted that she'd reach a point of being uncomfortable (again, I suspect an ultra runner's understatement) – but it no longer felt like it would be the worst that could happen. So with a sense of control she could put aside the unsettling all or nothing, succeed or fail fears that previously held sway.

In so doing, our third element in confidence comes to the fore: the feeling of *fluency* and everything coming together in the moment. We can see this – extraordinarily – at the 70-mile mark in the Grand Union Canal where Kat barely stopped at the aid station, so good was the feeling of running at her newfound, uninhibited pace.

It is perhaps worth saying that although Kat talks about her switch as a very definite, before and after revelation, it could not have happened without the hundreds of miles covered in previous events and training. Nor did it come about in a consciously thought through way, as if persuaded by reason. There was something far more intuitive and deeply felt: in her *being and body*, not just her brain.

This links to a recurrent theme we have seen in the book: the qualities of feeling and knowing. We've seen *knowing in action* as being able in the moment to spontaneously, before the words, respond creatively and in tune with the athlete or athletes in front of us. Similarly, Kat initially said her confidence switch was hard to explain and put into words – yet it was so deeply felt and known in the moment and beyond.

Here I want to make a distinction between our approach and some of the more popularized Sports Psychology. Possibly influenced by the problem-solving appeal of cognitive behavioural therapy, with its emphasis on language and the stories we tell ourselves, in some of its simplistic uses we might be told to encourage a nervous athlete to swap the words "scared", "fearful", "anxious" for positives like "excited". Indeed we are all for excitement. Yet Kat's story shows that the kind of excitement, calming composure and fluency we want to seek out, truly know and be changed by in a sustainable way, are found in a deeper, felt experience. And that the words follow behind.

We'll leave Kat for now as she carries on running ahead – meeting her again in Chapter 8 on resilience to learn more from her experiences at two later events: completing the Dragon's Back on her second attempt and the legendary Spartathlon. For now, let's give some structure to the conversations with those we coach as they prepare for their own big, daunting challenge or event.

The Four Ps of Confidence-Centred Coaching

I have found the following give some useful prompts and questions to explore with an athlete as they prepare for an event they have peaked for, or a particularly tough challenge ahead – easy to remember as the Four Ps of Confidence-Centred Coaching.

The Four Ps of Confidence-Centred Coaching:
Prompts for conversations

Place:	Past:
• out of place and belonging • reshaping the space and switching	• journeys and baggage • creating a new story
Present:	Paths:
• layered objectives • bringing the finish line to the start	• spirals and their undoing • scripts and self-talk

Place

Our first P is *place*. We'll look at two aspects: first, the feeling of being *out of place*; then, in more detail, how we can *reshape the space*.

We have already seen in Chapter 3: Confident coaches the importance of how, as coaches, we create our own spaces within which we can feel assured and bring out the best in ourselves and those we coach. The same is true for our athletes – to move from a sense of being unsure and hesitant, maybe overwhelmed by all that is around to a steadying, affirming their rightful place in what is about to unfold.

We will see at the end of this chapter, amongst those who come to me for help are some who have never swum – in their terms – "properly", yet yearn to enjoy and find a freedom in open water swimming. They often feel they don't belong in the same pool as so-called "real" swimmers, as if anyone had more right to be there. Why do we give ourselves such a hard time in the very things we most want to do?

Perhaps the answer for some lies deeper than it is the rightful place for a coach to delve into. As outlined in Chapter 4: Confidence in the coach, I believe that we can have an enormously positive effect by the simple generous act of treating the ambitions and aspirations of the person in front of us with the highest respect and regard – as a precious gift we are privileged to share in. Simply, in this way, without being consciously aware of it, we are effectively showing we believe the person before us has a rightful place alongside all the other "proper" and "real" aspirants.

And what of when the fateful day of a competition or challenge arrives? I think of my own experience and how intimidating and overwhelming a major event – like a big triathlon, a city marathon or long-distance swim – can feel, even if I tell myself I'm in the best shape of my life. All the noise and hype. So many people, all of them seeming to know what they are doing, some seriously scary, others relaxed and jovial, both heightening my nervousness. And as for the expensive kit on show! If it wasn't clear before, I'm now definitely sure that everything is telling me I really don't belong in this place.

Yet this is our place. What if we encourage those we coach to pause a moment on arrival, to take in the wonder of simply being there? How brilliant, after all the training, to know they are a part of what is about to unfold, alongside everyone else!

Here's where we can also begin *reshaping the space*, borrowing some useful tools from Sports Psychology. One of these is called switching. In those moments of feeling overwhelmed at a big event, it is as if I am being impacted on two fronts. There is the vastness of all that is out there and now pressing in on me: it's all *wide* and *external*. Yet what if we could train ourselves and those we coach, in those very moments, to switch the focus to the *narrow* and *internal?*

For the nervous novice open water swimmer looking out at the immensity of the sea before them, the big rolling waves or maybe the hundreds of competitors careering fearlessly into the water, it might be a narrowing of their focus: to the first buoy, the feet of the swimmer ahead, the water just ahead where their hands enter or the little pocket of air to the side. *External* to *internal* might be as simple as taking some composed deep breaths, reminding themselves about all the training they have done or recalling how their journey started so many months or years ago.

At other times it might be that a switch from narrow and internal to wide and external will come into its own. I find that, no matter how well prepared and fuelled up with magical mixes of isotonic drinks I am, at some point on a long swim I will get a cramp. A big, nasty, debilitating, shooting cramp. It doesn't always work but I've found it certainly helps to switch all that sudden, painful focus on one very specific, narrow part of my body to something wide and beyond: the beauty of the river all around, colours on the water, the flailing arms of a group of swimmers just ahead like something from a nature programme. The distraction certainly helps though I sense there's also something calming and reassuring, even in moments of pain, of relocating myself in the wider, wonder-filled space.

Before any big event I ask those I am coaching to draw up for themselves a grid: narrow/wide and internal/external. I suggest they fill in each quadrant with things they might focus on. Then, on their next swims, rides or runs, rehearse switching from one to the other, through all four quadrants. A kind of agile visualization – way more beneficial than fixing only on imagining crossing the line at the end.

The example shown – purely for indicative purposes – comes from some work with a highly competitive Great Britain triathlete who was getting into a spiral of unease and anxiety when racing on her time trial bike. Beth knew the bike in theory would enable her to keep up with the best but having witnessed another rider fall at speed, she found herself increasingly hesitant and unable to push hard. Perhaps better to leave the fancy bike at home and ride on something more stable. Worth saying, we are in the realm of super-light precarious machines, built for speed and not a secure sense of safety!

An illustrative switching grid: Beth on a time trial bike

	Narrow	Wide
External	The space just in front of my wheel The next road marking/lamppost The cyclists just ahead I'm lining up to overtake	The open road and countryside all around The buzz, excitement and energy of spectators
Internal	My ankles and legs turning with each pedal stroke How tucked in and aerodynamic am I! How cool I look in Ray-Bans	Being wholly present – right place, right time Everything working together in sync and rhythm Body and bike as one

The point is not so much *what* Beth chose for her particular focal points – it is developing the mental dexterity to switch through what might help in the moment, rehearsing these on training rides, runs and swims to the point where they are primed to switch as needed. In that way those we coach become adept at actively reshaping and reframing the place with all its tensions, pressures and potentially unsettling intrusions.

And it worked. Beth won her very next race and – best of all – felt comfortable on the bike and hungry for more.

Past

Remember Hannah showing up for her first track session in the last chapter? How in that moment she brought with her a whole bundle of very immediately, deeply felt emotions – everything overwhelmingly new, unsure where to go or how she would be received. Now think how much more potent a mix of the past is brought to a major event someone has spent months, maybe years preparing for.

There will be the immediately preceding past – a stressful journey to arrive in time, maybe a surprisingly tiring day before spent registering and nervously killing time. And at a deeper level there are sure to be ingrained self-doubts and fears. There's nothing like what Brené Brown would call "entering the arena" to heighten our sense of vulnerability, questioning whether we are really ready for what lies ahead, good enough to be there. Similarly, Performance Psychologist Pippa Grange, in her book *Fear Less*, suggests that at heart we are all driven by fear: a *"not-good-enough* fear… mixed up with what happened in the past and what might happen in the future"[31].

Now, here is where I think coaches have to be very clear about our limits and boundaries. As we talk things through, some of those I coach become aware of how past events or difficult times in their upbringing have impacted deeply on them. Whilst I will always want to offer an attentive listening ear, it's very important not to overstep the mark between coach and counsellor. As someone who has benefited enormously from the expert, professional care of psychotherapists and counsellors, I can resolutely say coaches are not and never should try to be therapists – no matter how compassionate, concerned for those we coach or well intentioned we may be.

I have found that Carol Dweck's notion of fixed and growth mindsets offers a safe and, in a sense, carefully bounded way of helping someone we coach explore for themselves their past, deep-rooted preconceptions and attitudes. Just to recap, Carol Dweck[32] suggested there can be significant differences in how we typically approach challenging tasks and the attitudes, our self-belief (or otherwise) and assumptions we tend to make about our abilities. These get reinforced, ingrained and played out in the way we talk.

In the case of our nervous novices who say before even starting they are "rubbish" and will never be "real" or "proper" athletes, I have found recounting fixed and growth mindsets enormously effective. When someone is starting to berate themselves about why they are not instantly getting a new technique, we can emphasize that we are learning something new, something that calls for patient persistence and a readiness to learn, maybe suggesting they add that wonderfully powerful word: "I can't do this… *yet.*"

And so to the athlete's big event or challenge, with the undermining past threatening to intrude and steal the day, we can also highlight the same

---

31 P. Grange *Fear Less: How to win at life without losing yourself* (2020).
32 C.S. Dweck *Mindset: How you can fulfil your potential* (2012).

growth mindset emphasis on "newness", the quality of a never been done before adventure. In this way we anchor their experience in the excitement, the thrilled anticipation of what is to come. In recent years, to help overcome my frustrations at my slowing with age I have sought out events I've not tried before, looking for new challenges free of any previous performance to judge myself against. Or if I am returning to an old favourite like a big river swim I might look out for the novelty – different conditions, different preparation – that makes comparing with previous times meaningless (or so I try to tell myself!).

And on the theme of creating something new, I have found it can help to suggest that a big looming event is a story about to be written: a kind of bringing the past into the future. Making memories is another way to think of this – the creation of something that is in effect a new "past" to be looked back on in future with a big grin.

One of the athletes I'd been working with, Brent, gave this suggestion an interesting twist on the long, gruelling bike ride in his first ever Ironman triathlon. Through each of the seven hours when he was tackling a very hilly course Brent imagined that at the 20-minute mark the local radio station would get in touch to forewarn him of an impending interview. At the 40-minute mark of each hour he would imagine they had said what the questions would be for his interview (probably around the theme of "How's it going out there?"). And then on each hour he would play out in his mind giving the interview, telling the story of his journey, of how he came to be there; how everything was coming together in that moment, the scenery, other cyclists, the looming hill or steep descent; and how the distance to the end was shortening each time. An in action switching of past, present and future. And of course it made for a great story to tell afterwards.

We will see more of this future-present-past in our next P.

Present

This is all about how those who we coach define for themselves the present challenge. Carol Dweck's notion of fixed and growth mindsets is again very relevant – the stark, win or lose, succeed or fail mentality typical of a fixed mindset creates even more pressure on what is already feeling like a formidable challenge. "Will I be thought of as failing – or think of myself as having failed – if I don't achieve what is expected?"

One way to take the edge off that inhibiting, all or nothing sense of a challenge is *layered objectives*. I suggest to those preparing for a big event, like a long-distance triathlon or a marathon, that they think through for themselves a layered sequence of aims that will make the event special to them. They are likely already to have in mind one particular goal, such as "simply" to get to the end or to break a specific time. The "simply" is in inverted commas as there is nothing simple or immediately obvious about the deeper hopes they might carry.

I remember my layered objectives for an Ironman started with an aim of finishing and enjoying it. In my heart though I knew I wouldn't be satisfied unless I not only finished and enjoyed it but also ducked below a certain time. And how amazing, in my dreams, if everything came together on the day and I broke an even faster time. This helped in the long, wearisome bordering on obsessive build-up of training and then on the day. In moments when I was really struggling, feeling I was too far beyond what I could do, I reminded myself of the finish-and-enjoy aim. And with that came a "If you can just keep going, Mike, you'll be able to get to the end a bit quicker than if you stopped and walked." Before long I surprised myself to realize I was well within my first time goal. And although the fastest time remained out of reach, I can look back at the whole experience with a quiet satisfaction and happy grin. Nice one, Mike.

A second idea for defining a present challenge is what I call *bringing the finish line to the start* – which we briefly touched on in Chapter 2: Rethinking confidence. Perhaps visually this makes more immediate sense in the kinds of competitive races I coach. Yet from talking with coaches from various team sports, all of which have some kind of end point and tallying up of scores, the idea seems just as relevant and is being widely practised. You hear it in the way the former Liverpool football manager the irrepressible Jurgen Klopp talked avidly about the fluency and commitment shown by his team and then, maybe with a shrug of the shoulders, disarmingly said that "Sure, a win would have been nice" and gave respect to the other team. Across so many sports the idea of what happens in the very moment of the match, game, play… is taking hold as the defining quality of success, what excites and elevates – with the end results taking care of themselves. What Pippa Grange would call *"winning deep"* as opposed to *"winning shallow"* and Cath Bishop *"winning long"*[33].

---

[33] C. Bishop *The Long Win: There's more to success than you think* (2024).

With the athletes I coach, *bringing the finish line to the start* means, first, taking in all that has been done to get there: ready, excited, poised to bring all the long training hours and the skilful, mindful preparation to the start. How extraordinary is that? Not every endurance athlete gets to be there, brought down by over-use injury or maybe an unwillingness to even contemplate such a challenge. So we take in the achievement of being there.

Then I suggest thinking of the space between the start line and the finish as – in the wonderful phrase from Michael Gervais and Pete Carroll – where they can create their *living masterpiece*. Like a blank canvas waiting to be filled with the most vibrant, living self-expression of all that they have worked on and brought to the moment. And times and places really do have a way of taking care of themselves, athletes surprised – sometimes stunned – by what they can do.

Paths

So we've looked at place, past and present. Our final P is *paths*.

Remember the painful story of my 5km championship race from Chapter 2? Well, some 40 years on and I'm taking part in one of the regular parkruns and I catch myself going down another really unhelpful, critical mental path. I'm somewhere around halfway in the long stream of runners and joggers and thinking how, back in my younger days, I would be way, way out in front. I've been overtaken by three people pushing their young children in fancy run pushchairs and a man with a dog. The last straw is being passed by people with what I'm thinking (in rather judgemental terms) are terrible run styles. Everything is starting to hurt and there's the beginnings of a self-defeating diatribe going on in my head: "What on earth am I doing here?! How can I be this slow? My calves are hurting. Everything is hurting! Why don't I just stop? Maybe at the next lap – or right here?"

But what if I could consciously choose another mental path? Maybe one more generous to those around me: "How amazing that so many people are out running! How brilliant to see all styles and shapes!"

I might even decide to say something positive to at least three people who pass me: "Wow – looking good! Go, go, go!"

Or the path could be one that starts with some kindness to myself: how brilliant to be here, still running all these years on from my heyday. I might focus on my form – am I relaxed in the upper body, light on my feet, pushing off the back foot? Or I might consciously look around and take in the wonder of my surroundings – the people, the scenery, the feel of the wind, sun or rain.

The key is to be able to spot the path we are going on or the thought pattern we fall into repeating – and then to make a conscious switch. And at that point what some Sports Psychologists call *scripts* or *self-talk* can come into play – though note once again the *knowing* comes before the words, not the other way round.

On to our big, daunting event and the following script examples are purely indicative. With each athlete facing their own personal challenges I suggest the following process – with thanks to Sport Psychologist Noe Orozco, from the GB Olympic and Paralympic triathlon programmes, for first introducing me to the approach. We first think through what are going to be the critical, potentially overwhelming moments. From there we map out a grid and the athlete thinks about what they might say to themselves in those moments that have a *tactical*, a *motivational* and a *technical* purpose. I then encourage the athlete to rehearse these in their longest or most intensive training sessions or to visualize themselves in those places, honing and refining their mantras ready for the moment.

An illustrative scripts grid: Mark at the Marathon des Sables

	At the start line each day	When it hurts	When the unexpected happens/ things go wrong
Tactical	My pace – no one else's	Keep going to the next x... and the one after	Break it down like a puzzle, one bit at a time
Motivational	Another day – and I'm here!	This is hard – and I do hard things	I can work this out
Technical	Check everything once, twice, three times through	One pole, one step, one pole, one step...	Stop. Breathe. Sort it.

Here's one that an athlete I coached for the famous six-day ultra run through the Sahara Desert, the Marathon des Sables, came up with. Mark knew from talking with previous contestants and from knowing his competitive instincts that he would really struggle each morning, no doubt after a broken, uncomfortable sleep. How would he drag himself to the start line, have the presence of mind to ensure the essential kit was ready and then not to be caught up or left desolate by the speedier runners? We also knew that there would be times when everything would hurt. Badly. And we knew things would go wrong at some point.

To pull out a few examples, Mark devised a tactical mantra to say at the start line as a check on himself: "My pace". The only one I suggested was a motivational phrase for when it was really hurting: "This is hard – and I do hard things" (with thanks to my partner who first suggested something similar). Notice it's not a "grit your teeth and get on with it" type of bludgeoning yourself through it motivation, which is only likely to add to the sense of pressure. There's an acknowledgement of the suffering – and a sense of affirming this is the place to be. And being an engineer, he had a set of problem-solving mantras to be able calmly to work his way through any unexpected mishaps (of which there were quite a few!).

So there are our Four Ps of Confidence-Centred Coaching – simple prompts to talk through and help guide an athlete to prepare for a big event. Each will be different as every place, past, present challenge and thought pattern is unique to each athlete.

And finally

One final act remains. The event is over: nothing more can be done, living masterpieces behind the athletes, and rich, meaning-filled memorable stories crafted. Too often when the race or event is over we assume our job is done and our attention turns to other athletes we are coaching and the next challenges ahead. Or perhaps it's straight on to the next game or match, as if hastily moving on and away from what has just happened. Where is the athlete left?

In the big events I help athletes undertake, this is another key moment. Having focused so single-mindedly on a big event, now it is behind them, many will feel an emptiness and lack of purpose. Perhaps doubts come in: "What if I had pushed that bit harder?" or "If only I hadn't messed up on a particular point". The masterpiece starts to feel somehow incomplete or not as good as it might have been. And so another goal is quickly set. It is very common to hear of athletes who, on completing their biggest event, like an Ironman triathlon, have already registered for another the following year before they have even got home from the first.

How important to make the time and space to relive with those we coach their experience of the event – whatever the result. To sit together and let them talk the whole experience through, every detail recounted: from the journey to the event, registering, setting up, lining up at the start and each memorable moment of the event itself to what they did and how they felt afterwards. You might think of this as a coach helping frame their masterpiece then standing back, pausing a while to take in together the depth and colour of what has been created. As if looking deeply at a work of art, absorbing ourselves in its overall impact as well as the finer details. There it is, an unrushed, private viewing for the coach and coached, artistic director and artist – and note, without any judgement of times, positions or other external criteria.

> "What I've wanted to talk about… is that very sense of amazement, about the strong desire (or will, you might say) *to hold on to the purity of that feeling of amazement.*"
>
> Haruki Murakami (emphasis added)[34]

Can this work in team sports where there may be a packed season of games and matches, one fixture following within days of another? Perhaps not with the same depth, given the pressure of time – yet therein lies the challenge: to make time to stay connected to the experience. And note: this is not about going straight to lessons learnt or what would be done differently next time. Sit silently with the masterpiece. Like author Murakami, writing about being a novelist over many years, *hold on to that purity of feeling amazement.*

And for us here, after all the ultra running and the exhaustion of the big events, it's time to stop, attend to our aching muscles and spend some time with a physio – not just any physio though. The following reflections come from several conversations with Dr Jo Gladwin, a Consultant Physiotherapist.

---

[34] From H. Murakami (translated by P. Gabriel and T. Goosen) *Novelist as a Vocation* (2024).

Jo brings to her practice a deep interest in mindfulness and how we can reconnect to our bodies to find healing and hidden strengths. And she happens to be someone I coached for her first big open water swimming events. So her own journey through self-doubt and becoming a strong, in tune swimmer gives an extra set of insights into the themes of this chapter: confidence as a knowing in our being and bodies before the words.

Reflective Conversation: Knowing in the body with Dr Jo Gladwin

I first met Jo when she came for an open water swim lesson. A one-time speedy runner and racket sports aficionada, in her mind, swimming was always something others did. Living by the coast she felt the pull of the water, admired from afar the groups of early-morning dippers and found herself wanting to discover what it would be like to be one of them. No great distances or epic events in mind – more a sense of wonder-filled wondering how it would be to be a "real" swimmer. And something to prove to her family – and herself – but not quite sure what.

She got in touch with me, initially for a one-to-one lesson and then to work together on some super challenges – at first feeling a 1km event would be beyond her. She then set her sights on a challenging SwimRun event in Snowdonia, a 6km open water swim and is now excited at the prospect of even bigger challenges and adventures to come.

Our conversations often stray into the parallels and crossovers with learning to swim and the work she does with patients in her physiotherapy practice. We both share a view of confidence and wellbeing as things that are rooted in a wholeness and deeper feelings that we experience and truly know. No quick fixes, being connected in one's body and the skilful art of listening to oneself and others are recurrent themes. So some rich insights to close this chapter on coaching for confidence.

Out of place and finding an inner space

In the earlier days, though, it was noticeable how often our conversations would centre around her feelings of not being a "proper swimmer". At times she cut short sessions, not out of tiredness, more from feeling unnerved and intimidated by others, ploughing up and down or basking at the end of the lane as if they owned the place. I would point out that she had just as much a right to be there, having paid the same entry fee. And that the "proper" swimmer doesn't really exist – they are figments of our self-limiting mindsets that tell us we shouldn't be in the same pool or stretch of water. We are – no less, no more – the swimmer that we choose to be.

Yet no matter how much she agreed with these sentiments and even berated herself for thinking in a self-limiting way, the sense of being out of place persisted. Nor did her developing fitness, her steady progress in covering greater distances or even successfully accomplishing first one kilometre then one mile in open water seem to make a significant shift (in the way Kat talked of her before and after "confidence switch").

Revealingly, Jo gradually started to shift away from that "out of place" feeling as she became more sensitized and attuned to herself in the water – the finding and losing herself in the moment that is a theme throughout this book, whether to do with the coach or athlete. The *knowing in action* we saw in Chapter 2: Rethinking confidence. A natural mindfulness, rooted in being attuned to *form*, *effort* and *movement* rather than swimming with a head full of instructions or target times and distances.

Perhaps there is something deeper, then, than the kind of agile external/ internal switching of focus we looked at for our athletes in those moments of feeling overwhelmed by everything around them, much as that has real value. It is as if the outer intrusions somehow fell quietly into place – something for her to no longer feel intimidated by. Instead she found that the inner sensations of being at one in the water, in her own rhythm and revelling in discovering the swimmer in her, increasingly grounded her experience and excited her. And when she told me about her swims, the people coming and going at different speeds and varying degrees of splashy-ness, it was more with a laugh as an amusing side story to her own sensation-rich swim.

Body and mind connections

This links into a related theme in our conversations, more to do with her own practice. I was struck by her telling me that many of the people she sees in her work seem disconnected from or out of tune with their bodies. A patient will come and talk about their condition as if it were an isolated point in their body that has gone wrong and needs a targeted fix. I have to admit in the past I would go and see physios looking for a specific tightness to be ironed out or an over-use injury to be treated quickly so I could get back to training or competing, as if it were somehow detached from the rest of me. I never bluntly said "Just get this bit of me fixed so I can get back to what I was doing before" but that was my agenda – no time for a deeper listening to how I felt in body and mind.

Jo told me that over many years of practice she has become more attuned to and aware of how a patient, maybe entering her consulting room for the first time, carries themselves – a stooped weariness and sense of being beaten; or perhaps a brittle fragility in just about holding it together. The impression I had is of her being more in tune with the whole person before her than sometimes they are with themselves. And interestingly she emphasizes the importance of the patient being the one who does the restorative work, not her.

This again makes me wonder about the "fix-it" nature of some popularized Sports Psychology, presented as top tips and techniques to overcome isolated, narrowly conceived problematic thinking as if that were detached from the whole person. The psychologist prescribes and the athlete's neatly demarcated problem should be sorted – so long as they follow the expert advice. Of course our own Four Ps might fall into the same trap of being seen as formulaic, coach-led prescriptions.

Yet this is the reason for the emphasis on open conversations with athletes, questioning, listening and evoking from them what they find works, feels true and meaningful to them. How could it be otherwise? When absolutely full out, top speed, hunched down on the time trial bike and a cross wind hits? With two marathons run in two days already and a whole day and night of running for 50 miles through the Sahara lies ahead? When preparing for a long river swim that, less than a year before would have seemed utterly impossible and only for the ridiculously able "proper" swimmers? (Go, Dr Jo, go!)[35]

Back to listening

One final reflection on our super conversations. I asked Jo about what she feels in herself when a patient enters her consulting room. She talked about how her awareness of the way someone is carrying themselves doesn't just come from observation but is somehow transferred to her and felt in her

---

[35] And go she did, completing both the 6km Bantham Swoosh and an epic SwimRun event in Snowdonia.

own body – not the specific point of pain or injury, more the general sense of tension, distrust or anxiety. A kind of empathy in the body that goes to the deeper, underlying state of what the patient brings into the room.

And I asked, in such a moment, with her intuitive feeling for a patient who seems disconnected, how she helps them begin to attune themselves in the more rounded, mind and body in sync way. "By listening," she said. By her giving the unhurried time and attentive space, it is as if patients can start listening to themselves and connect to their deeper, underlying feelings that will be key to the restorative process. Sound familiar?

So what can we take into Part 3 of the book from the realm of coaching for confidence? Here are some suggestions:

- the extraordinary joy and life-affirming experience of people surprising themselves with what they can do – what greater purpose and reward for a coach can there be?

- the difference between shallow and deep – contrast quick fixes and easy formulas with a slower, more painstaking and patient exploring of what is truly meaningful and felt in the athlete's and our own whole being. Where do you want your coaching to be?

- when it's done, a hushed taking in of the profound beauty of stories created, magical masterpieces of the moment and experiences rich in meaning that we are so privileged to share

- how the all-important connections – which enable both those we coach and us as coaches to find ourselves at our best – start with attentive listening: listening to others and to ourselves, coached and coach. What a powerful and deeply skilful art to practise and ground our coaching for confidence in.

The next part of the book takes us into coaching in the changed landscape that has opened up for us. We will see how key issues and challenges that occupy attention in the coaching world take on a very different form and shape to how they are typically thought of:

- how creativity becomes a fundamental and defining feature of coaching all ages, abilities and ambitions

- how conventional wisdom and models of motivation are turned on their heads, revealing something far more intricate and engaging

- likewise, we will come to a deeper, almost humbling view of resilience than is typically found

- colouring everything is a kindness in how we look after ourselves, with far-reaching implications for the places we coach in.

Ready to go there?

Part 3
Coaching in a changed landscape

6
The magic of creativity

"Music crosses my path like a figure that makes me curious, challenges and touches me… Together [with pianist François Couturier] we search as if through various countries, exploring, shaping, struggling, rejecting and finding new forms to finally sing the song."

Anja Lechner[36]

THIS NEXT PART of the book will look in turn at four big topics in coaching: the artistry and magic of creativity; motivation and inner drives; the mysteries of resilience; and protecting our energy. By rethinking our understanding of confidence and its place in all we do, we open up a whole new perspective on how each of these is thought of, the principles and practices we want to make our own and the impacts we can have. And each stands out as a key feature of our changed landscape to coach in.

We start with a theme running through the book: creativity. In what still counts for many as "normal" coaching, with the coach as the expert imparting their knowledge to compliant athletes, we might think of creativity as something a bit quirky and off the wall. From a safe distance we might admire those coaches who seem to come up with wild and wonderful ideas, marvelling at their ingenuity and bravura, whilst quietly telling ourselves it's

---

[36] From liner notes for A. Lechner and F. Couturier *Lontano* ECM Records (2020).

not for us. Or some will think of creativity as fun, playful downtime once they are done with the "proper" coaching. And even amongst the growing number of coaches who, to powerful effect, integrate games into fun-based sessions with young people, the assumption is often that playful activity and the use of games have little relevance when we move on to coaching adults. When we hear of coaches encouraging their players to "Just go and enjoy yourselves", "Have fun", maybe evoking something of that playfulness they might have had in much younger days, it is often with a kind of if-all-else-fails resignation, having tried every other way.

In contrast, we are going to put creativity right at the very heart of our coaching: a key defining feature of the new landscape we want to move into. And for coaching at every level, ambition and ability, and for every age. Here is coaching at its very best and most rewarding – where there is a creative interplay, the coach and coached sharing in making something new and fresh that has a depth and energy of its own and leaves both enriched. And we will see creativity has a powerful impact in unlocking real and sustained confidence and self-belief.

In this chapter we will:

- turn to some highly innovative young stars to illustrate something of the wonder of creativity in action

- draw on a helpful definition of creativity and then see it in practice in a busy, challenging coaching environment

- explore what gets in the way of us being creative

- finish with an inside view of a highly creative, participative process in our Reflective Conversation, with lessons for us in engagement.

And as we've done before, we will draw lessons and insights from outside of coaching as well as from the inner stories of coaches and coached.

One night in Camden

It is on the theme of drawing out an unexpected creativity from unlikely sources that we start with a trip to Camden, London.

A few years ago I enjoyed a wonderful evening at Scene & Heard, a unique mentoring project for young people of between 8 and 11 years old – many of whom have suffered some form of trauma or hardship. Scene & Heard teams the children up with drama specialists to write short plays which professional, adult actors then perform to a live audience. On the night I attended, each play followed a format of an interaction between two somewhat random objects or creatures, which then got disrupted or affected by a third. Underlying each play you could sense something of the children's own journeys – an escape to a better place; a way out of inertia or confusion to an exciting if still unknown future; a newfound perspective on troubled life. All played out with great humour and energy.

I came away moved and inspired by the evening – seeing the young playwrights gleefully, shyly taking a bow at the end of each of their amazing plays. In the audience there was a sense of disbelieving surprise which turned to captivation at such imaginative creations, all performed with dedication and professionalism by the actors. As each short story unfolded and was taken so far out of the ordinary, no limits seemed to be set on what each character could be like, who they might then meet up with or how their interactions would develop. Why not have a conversation between a multicoloured zebra and a psychopathic seashell? Why can't a granite rock have a personality and feelings? Why wouldn't a discarded grammar revision textbook bemoan the fact that it had yet to be opened? Why limit ourselves to the normal and the boundaries of what's always expected?

Now, creativity certainly includes an element of going beyond the expected, of imagining things differently and not just doing what we've always done. So in that respect, those coaches who get the athletes they coach to respond to new set-ups or rules – as we saw at the end of Chapter 3 in the Reflective Conversation with Tom Hartley and his re-inventing the rules for a football practice – are certainly on to something. I think we can also see something deeper going on in Scene & Heard. The super-imaginative creations were all underpinned and made possible by:

- an attentive listening to each young person, their stories and ideas

- an eager openness to go with the children's ideas, to explore them together and see where they would take the creator and audience

- everyone's clear, undivided focus on creating superb theatre.

And what extraordinary power such an attentive, caring, ideas-rich environment – of being *listened* to – had on the young playwrights' sense of self-worth. Their bashful grins shone through the night. And as the Scene & Heard website testifies, many of the young playwrights go on to careers in the performing arts.

Creativity defined

Time to be clear on what we mean by creativity. Not necessarily the wild and weird, though there's certainly an element of doing things differently. Nor something that only happens in the arts world or on select stages, though as we'll see with the following examples, there's much to learn from those in the creative arts. For our definition we turn to the late and very sadly missed, renowned expert on creativity Sir Ken Robinson.

> "My definition of creativity is 'the process of having original ideas that have value'."
>
> Ken Robinson[37]

There are three key ideas in this definition. First, it's a *process* – not some random, accidental happening that comes out of nowhere. Think of a painter readying themselves to practise their art. There's an uncluttering, a clearing of the mind to focus on what is before them, a searching for a connection, looking more deeply each time to truly see what is in front of them. There is also an all-important element of bringing themselves to the work, who they are, as if engaging with the subject. Their creativity lies not in producing an identical replica of what is before them but in how they perceive and sense what is there, and in that very process they show something of themselves.

We see some of that process in Scene & Heard: the attentive care and listening, allowing a space to explore ideas and the dedicated focus. The same should hold true for our own coaching: connections rooted in being wholly present, a deep respect and regard for the person in front of us, an inquisitiveness and shared sense of excitement about the possibilities that lie ahead. And note: this is a skilful, learnable process, not random coincidence or the preserve of a few free-thinking mavericks or beyond-reach stellar coaches.

Second, there is an *originality*, in the sense of actively looking to develop something new each time – beautifully captured in Anja Lechner's depiction of searching in foreign lands to arrive at a new form of singing a song. I also think of the way a jazz supremo interacts with the other members of their band and their audience. They might start with the familiar refrains

---

[37] From K. Robinson with L. Aronica *The Element: How finding your passion changes everything* (2009).

of a well-known tune – then the interplay between them somehow leads to something spontaneous and flowing as they get into the swing, letting the music take over, each time expressive of different emotions and moods, rhythms or phrasing. (I'm a big fan of jazz trios!) And note, we are not in the realm of make-it-up-as-you-go-along improvisation (though perhaps some of the music I like does stray that way) – but rather a readiness to let go of set formats and see what new creations emerge.

Imagine approaching every coaching encounter with an excited anticipation to see what might unfold, an openness to new experiences and lessons, looking for the music of coaching to take over. How much more fulfilling and rewarding than just repeating past practice and ways of doing things, no matter how successful they might have been or how much we convince ourselves they are the "right way".

And third, there is an element of *value*. For those we coach this might be in terms of a newfound proficiency, a joy in the fluency and everything coming together in the moment or in the end results. For the coach the value might be in terms of our learning and satisfaction at having tried something different and seen how it works. In both cases it is clear there will also be a real benefit in terms of self-belief and a readiness to try other novel ways of doing things.

There are two other points to note. In Ken Robinson's words "You can be creative in anything at all – anything that involves using your intelligence." Anything. How we coach, teach, address problems and challenges, our relationships… And *anyone can be creative*. Creativity is not limited to a few gifted, "arty" people (much as there are some extraordinarily imaginative, talented individuals out there). If creativity is a process that hinges around the actions we have highlighted, then it is within each and every one of us to develop as a skilful, personal practice.

Creativity in practice

So what might this look like and how might we go about being creative in our coaching sessions? Let's go back to the busy swim session at our local tri club that we left toward the end of Chapter 3.

It's another week and there's the usual busy commotion of people coming and going, chatting amongst themselves and catching up with whatever is on their minds. Some will be visibly carrying the stresses of the day: of rushing from one place to another or the pressure of responding to endless demands at home or work. There's an edgy air of a passive yet impatient "Just tell us what we're doing and we'll get on with it." Or maybe for some a resigned, low expectation that what's coming will be an hour of struggling to keep up, of not being very good. Something to endure in the half-hearted hope that an improvement might somehow come. Not the most promising material for a creative interplay.

I've found focusing on four points of *creative interaction* – making them the basics I want to get right and excel at every time – seems to allow for that free-flowing, spontaneous music of coaching to take over and brings great results. You will recognize them from all that we have seen in the book so far and in the Scene & Heard example above.

As always, it starts with a connection. As we saw, there's an all-important process of stilling our minds amidst all the commotion, of being wholly present and attentive to the person or people in front of us. To turn a point of contact into a connection. Remember the 10 and 2 rule from Chapter 4? Of having just 10 seconds, no more, to make someone feel welcome, then two minutes to set the tone for what will follow.

I also want to generate a sense of shared energy and engagement. As we saw the first time we coached at the session, back in Chapter 3, being really clear and succinct about the purpose of the session lifts my own coaching energy levels and makes me feel more assured. That in turn helps the group to focus and bring the best of themselves to the session. Our shared energy and engagement feed off each other and make the session flow.

For the avoidance of doubt, this is not about so-called "fake it till you make it". There is nothing fake in bringing our true selves to a session, nor in the act of sharpening our sense of purpose to engage with others. Genuine interest in others and being true to ourselves, as we discussed in Chapter 3, sets the ground for a dynamic engagement: athletes and coach immersed in a purposeful session and feeding off each other's energy.

And once that starts to happen I want to create a space in which we can explore together, trying out and experimenting with what works, what it feels like to make that extra effort, to adapt the technique, to push harder or be more relaxed, with more of a heightened feel for form, intensity of effort or movement. In this way the whole session becomes a series of *coaching moments*, seized upon to great effect. And asking all the time how something felt, before offering my observations, helps to underscore that it's a shared endeavour rather than a coach's test to pass or fail.

What does a coaching moment look like, there, at the pool with everyone swimming up and down their busy lanes? I might notice that someone seems to be making a big effort but not really moving in a fluent, composed way and that, for example, they seem flat in the water, putting a lot of effort into swinging their arms round, before a mighty splash. So picking a time when they have paused between sets, I first need to ask if they'd like a suggestion to try out and, if so, how they are feeling about their swimming. Depending on what they say, I might offer something like: "I wonder how it would be if you focus on rolling your body more with each stroke? It might make it easier to bring your arms over, and to spear your hands into the water. How about imagining you're now breathing from your hips so you get your whole body rotating as one?"

Now, having given a suggestion I need to be absolutely sure to be at the end of the lane, ready to ask "How was that? What did you feel?" Michael Gervais talks about coaching moments as the two to three seconds after someone has performed an activity. If I am not right there in those few seconds, showing a real interest and ready to respond with the simple "How was that?" who knows what the swimmer will have taken from what they tried?

And very typically when I am there, ready to find out, they will immediately ask "So how did I look?" No doubt somewhat irritatingly, my standard reply is always "Well, tell me first how it felt." Only after listening to how it felt, whether there was a difference, how natural or unnatural it felt, maybe asking for some specific detail – like "Could you feel a difference in your hands as they entered? Anything else?" – might I say something along the lines of "I think there's more to come, so worth seeing how much further we can take it" or "To me, you seemed more relaxed and certainly faster" and "Hang on to that feeling through the rest of the session and let's see how it goes."

One more point of creative interplay and it's what I think of as *banking*. Most sessions – certainly club swim sessions – tend to finish with everyone keen to get out, get changed and be quickly on their way. Before they do, we can do at least two things to capture and, as it were, bank what we have worked on.

One is to finish the session with a short section that challenges swimmers on the technique we have been focusing on, thereby bringing us back to the purpose of the session. Another is simply asking people as they leave about a specific coaching point – "How did it feel? What difference did it make?" – and thereby prompting them to reflect on what worked, ready to take into their next session. It also helps underline that we are engaged in a shared endeavour. And, needless to say, provides me with some feedback on what has or hasn't worked.

Now, imagine someone going home after a swim session where the coach, as typically happens, has picked up on some flaw and given corrective instruction:

"How was your swim session, darling?"

"Okay, I suppose. Bit knackering."

A weary pause.

"I don't know if it's worth all the effort – I'm still pretty much stuck in the same place. The coach said I should 'rotate' more... I tried but I'm not sure I really got it. Hopefully next week he can tell me if I'm doing it right or not, but it's hard to get his attention as it's such a busy session."

"Sorry about that. By the way, don't forget we're going out tomorrow night."

Yet what if we approached the session as an interactive, creative endeavour, exploring what is possible and putting all our focus on those precious, two to three second coaching moments, asking the swimmer how they feel as they try out our suggestions? I suspect the conversation back home would go very differently.

Without needing to be asked (and before even putting the swim bag down):

"Wow! That was so good! I think I've finally made a bit of a breakthrough. I tried this different way of rolling my whole body and I just felt like I was slicing through the water. I felt stronger and faster. It felt weird at first but then, wow, when it clicked! I can't wait to get back to the pool before the next session and keep working on it."

"Ah, that's great. And you haven't forgotten about tomorrow night, have you?"

What gets in the way

If creative coaching is a skill that almost anyone can learn, put into practice and develop, what is stopping us? The answer lies, I believe, in the *letting go* that has been a repeated theme throughout the book – letting go of positioning ourselves as the all-knowing expert and owner of the right way to do things; and letting go of the way we compare ourselves to others.

"Who owns the right way?"

There's a phrase we have touched on that I like to use in my coaching and with other coaches: "Who owns the right way?" If I want those I coach to feel for themselves the qualities that we identified in the last chapter – of being attuned to their own form, effort and movement – then how they look to even the most highly qualified, knowledgeable coach is less important. Way more important is their connection to themselves, the feelings they seek out and nurture, refine and make their own – just like the truly knowing in mind and body that we saw in ultra runner Kat and the Reflective Conversation with Consultant Physiotherapist Dr Jo. And remember Psychotherapist Margo Bristow's trusting belief in the young people she supports – her emphasis on the therapist "getting out of the way" and trusting in the wisdom and expertise of the young people before her.

When I was researching and preparing this chapter I had a very interesting exchange of ideas in a peer support group of coaches I belong to. I asked what creative coaching meant for each of them. Initially those more involved in coaching younger athletes talked about their use of games, sharing some super-inventive ideas. As our conversation developed, other coaches – more involved in working with adults and in high performance, competitive environments – began to reflect on what it felt like to go beyond the expected, to try new ideas and approaches. Needing to be *brave* and *patient* and having a *self-belief* were some of the qualities they began to identify and reflect on.

And of course if we see coaching as a creative interaction, where both coach and coached together explore what is possible and beyond, thereby creating something new, then we will feel exposed. Who knows what might happen? Or how quickly it might happen. We're meant to have all the answers, ready to hand, not leave it all up to the athlete to discover!

I remember sharing in another peer group "Who owns the right way?" with the focus on the athlete discovering and feeling for themselves what being at their best means, rather than us measuring them up against our view of the "right" effort, readings on a power meter or perfectly executed swim stroke. One of the coaches responded incredulously "Why would anyone come to us for coaching if it's all about what the athlete feels?"

Why indeed? Yet come they do – and find an absorbing, enriching sense of how good it can feel to lose and find themselves in the moment; a knowing in their bodies that comes into its own in the toughest of challenges; and a realization of deeper meaningfulness beyond what they originally were looking for. And my experience is that increasingly there is a real hunger for a different way of helping people find the inner swimmer, cyclist, runner – whatever the sport – that is yearning to come out, rooted in what they feel rather than how they measure up against some external criteria.

It might not work for everyone, but what a difference we can make for those who come to us! And I find having the courage to let go of positioning ourselves as the expert – always expected to be in the know, answers and prescriptions at the ready, the holder of the "right way" to perform – brings a deeply rewarding richness and constant freshness to each contact.

The curse of comparison

There is another act of letting go to enable us to be creative in our coaching (and pretty much every other area of our lives) and this one is highlighted by Brené Brown. In her groundbreaking book *The Gifts of Imperfection*[38], she sets out a series of what she calls Guideposts to the daily practices of wholehearted living. They are set out as opposite points on a series of spectrums, for example: a letting go of what people think and a moving toward or cultivating authenticity and being true to ourselves; a letting go of perfectionism and in its place cultivating self-compassion. It is very powerful – a must-read if you haven't already. Interestingly for us here, she positions the thing to let go of if we are to move to creativity as *comparison*.

"Comparison is the crush of conformity from one side and competition from the other – it's trying to simultaneously

---

[38] B. Brown *The Gifts of Imperfection* (2010).

fit in and stand out. Comparison says 'Be like everyone else, but better.'"

Brené Brown[39]

How can we be creative if we are constantly caught up in the pressure to fit in? And at the same time, somehow also be seen to be as good as or even better than others? Conforming and competing. I know this from moments in some of the most free-form, imaginative and joyful coaching and teaching I do: the swim sessions with disabled children that we looked at in Chapter 3. As I write this I'm thinking back to a recent session with a young, super-enthusiastic, if somewhat uncoordinated swimmer. We've been trying some swimming along the bottom of the pool, which I'm thinking might help develop a stronger sense of composed control and fuller arm movements to take into his swimming on the surface.

At one point in our last session we used a large submerged Hula Hoop ring, at first doing the obvious of swimming through it. He then spontaneously came up with a novel and challenging way to swim through it – how about together standing on it so it was held flat on the pool floor, on his command jumping back and as it righted itself seeing how quickly he could swim through it? Why not? "Let's give it a try," I said. It was great fun and helped him move more quickly than before, still not quite with the fuller arm movement I hoped for but achieving something he had not done before, capped with a massive grin as he came up for air.

Out of the blue I felt an uneasy doubt rise up – what would the other swim teachers, standing at poolside running their conventional lessons in the prescribed ways, think of our apparent larking about? Should I rein in the fun and conform to what would be expected of a so-called "normal" lesson? To do what swim teachers are meant to do? And how could I show any progress if it wasn't in improving a recognizable swim stroke, so many metres covered or swimming faster?

How much stronger and constricting is the pressure to conform to what is expected of coaches in a typical club environment, or even more so in high performance, elite or professional environments? Our training to qualify as coaches will almost certainly have laid out the roles and routines to be followed. The higher one goes in terms of the professional world

---

[39] B. Brown *Atlas of the Heart* (2021).

of coaching at an elite level, the more regimented, circumscribed, critically viewed and commented on will be what is expected of a coach – whether explicit in set procedures, plans and protocols or tacit in what everyone knows to be "how we do things round here". Worse still must be those all too common divisive environments where it's never really clear what we are meant to conform to and why some are "in" and others are out on the margins.

As introduced in the quote above, Brené Brown's research interestingly led her to juxtapose conformity with competition. How true in too many professional coaching environments. Coaching can be a pretty cutthroat, winner takes all business, with people jostling, elbowing each other out of the way for position. Even in clubs with volunteer coaches one can find oneself on the end of a misplaced jealousy as some coaches vie to be centre stage. An empty competition for attention that has no real winners disengages those who are made to feel undervalued and does anything but model the very behaviours we would want to see in those we coach. Truly a curse on creativity.

Before moving back to something more uplifting, it is worth making the point that we might be encouraged to "be creative", "take risks", "think outside the box." All commendable and definitely to be supported. But what is suggested here is not a jump into an "anything goes" randomness. Our approach firmly grounds our creativity in the process of being attentively focused, connecting with and being attuned to ourselves and others, bringing forward an engaging energy and then exploring the boundaries of what is possible – rich, deeply known and felt, and true to coach and coached.

Reflective Conversation: Creative imprint with Anne Colvin

And we will now see something of the magic that can be created as we turn to our next Reflective Conversation, this one with Dance Artist and Choreographer Anne Colvin – a pioneer of extraordinary practice in her field with much for us to learn from in ours. I have been lucky enough to see some of Anne's work up close and owe many of the ideas in this chapter and elsewhere in the book to her.

Over the last eight years or so, under the banner of imprint, Anne has been developing unique and captivating work inspired by people's connections with nature – different locations and different meaningful, personal connections. She has brought her approach to a wide range of settings and groups who would not typically be drawn to or able to access contemporary dance, such as women in recovery from drug or alcohol misuse or children at Great Ormond Street Hospital. One such project, just before the COVID-19 pandemic, brought together three professional dancers and several people from the Brighton Unemployed Centre Families Project (BUCFP).

Unlike ballet or many other forms of dance with very precisely prescribed choreography, contemporary dance in general allows for more of a creative development between choreographer and dancers, as they together explore expressive movement within the space. Anne takes that further, working with dancers and non-dancers, rooting what is created in their responses to the natural environment. And rather than confining her work to theatres or other traditional stages, performances might be out in the open, in nature itself – or in the case of Great Ormond Street Hospital, super-imaginative ways are found to bring nature to the children.

The process

The project with BUCFP started in a large studio space in Brighton. Anne brought together people from the centre who had shown an initial interest with her three dancers and a filmmaker. Over the course of two days they together explored each person's connections with nature – stories from childhood as well as more recent experiences, what was thought and felt, the imprints left. Each person captured their recollections and thoughts in the ways they felt most at ease with – some through drawing on a big, long roll of paper, others by creating collages of photos and prompts Anne had collected.

Then, over the following six weeks they went to a beautiful part of the South Downs, Devil's Dyke. On each visit they explored the woods and surrounding landscape and allowed themselves the time and space to take in whatever struck them, with Anne capturing their words and thoughts – the wind through the trees, the sense of opening perspectives from views up close to far-off rolling hills. Each person seemed to find something that connected to a deeper feeling – an unburdening of worries, a stilling sense of calm, a letting go and a being held, a childlike playfulness and an immersion in the grandeur of the space. Out of this came ideas for movements that expressed some of these sensations and reflections. The filmmaker, Matt Bartram, captured much of this in a short, sensitively shot film[40].

After several rainy day rehearsals, the dancers performed to an invited audience, turning Devil's Dyke into a grand, open air, windswept theatre. And coming full circle back to how the project started, the audience were asked to record the imprint the performance left on them on a big roll of paper laid out between the trees, under makeshift tarpaulin covers.

Behind the process

I talked with Anne about how she drew in her untrained dancers so they felt able not just to take part, but to give so much of themselves. How did she help bring out the undiscovered richness of expression that is captured in the film, in the voice-overs (some quoted here) reflecting on their experience and the apparent easiness and joy of their performance? How was she able to help the BUCFP members, with little or no experience in contemporary dance, move beyond "I could never do that" to expressing themselves in a deep, personally connected way that helped make the whole piece come alive?

"I can feel the strength of nature – it unleashed something."

"I feel at one in myself."

"I left my shell."

"Playing in the woods, as if dreaming in the wonderland. At this moment I lost my upset and forgot my pain."

"Looking up at the sky, bathing in the sun – I can sincerely say: 'It's good to be alive.'"

Selected voice-overs from imprint dancers

Anne emphasized the importance from the very outset of getting to know the participants, making time for *an unhurried interest* in each one. It was clear her interest was in each person – who they are rather than just as prospective dancers. Being genuinely keen to know about each person's stories and background helped engender a sense of trust and being valued.

---

[40] Available, along with other films and projects, at www.imprintcreative.org

You'll recognize the parallels with all that we looked at in Chapter 4 about connections and relationships of trust, being seen and listened to.

Such unhurried inquisitiveness and openness were also shown in the time set aside for all the dancers – individually and as a group – to take in, reflect on and share their experiences of their surroundings. Time was given over to connect to what they saw, heard, felt, the emotions it provoked, touching something deep within each of them.

A second point Anne gave special weight to was to start – and keep coming back to – her deeper *purpose*, rather than going into the detail of how she might want the work to look or what would be correct technique. My sense, watching occasionally from the sidelines, was of a respectful listening to each other. I could see everyone involved in creating something together, without a right way to follow or set dance techniques to conform to. When questions arose about more technical, detailed aspects, or things weren't quite coming together, Anne brought the focus back to the spirit or feeling that the group wanted to express. A great reminder to me of the importance of connecting to a deeper purpose, such as the confidence and self-belief to reach for a new height of speed, endurance, fluency or strength – rather than jumping straight to prescribe a certain technique or programme of training to be followed.

Finally, something I saw – and which was picked up and commented on by others – was Anne's *selfless generosity and trusting belief* in her performers. Anne didn't make herself the centre of the creative work – though she clearly was the originator, carefully guiding everything along and occasionally lifting everyone's energy or calling for a time-out to reflect and rest. And making the focus each dancer's deepening journeys somehow had a profound effect on their self-belief. You can see this in some of the quotes here. One of the participants said to me after their performance "That's the best day of my life – best thing I've ever done."

"It's been quite mind blowing because when you're stuck in your own little world, this brings you out. Walk. Have a laugh. And take down the shell. Take the wall away – that's what we've done. And individually you feel 'wow' and you walk away and you feel better."

One might think this is to do with Anne's personality, not wanting to be centre stage, and to a degree that may be true – I recognize a similar modesty and hesitancy in myself. But a lesson I take goes back to the process. Anne devised a way of working that is rooted in others' experiences. And her generosity and belief in the artists – much like Margo's belief in her young clients' wisdom – ripples all the way through.

So what can we take into the new emerging landscape of coaching? We go back to a point on coaching circles from Chapter 1. In the sports coaching world we like to use the phrases "athlete-centred" and "co-creation" – but it has to be said that the practice doesn't always follow the rhetoric. The shape of an athlete-centred coaching world remains indistinct and blurred by so much of the conventional, old-world way of doing things. And co-creation, for all the great intentions, can sometimes feel like an awkward dance between mismatched partners.

In imprint and Scene & Heard I see a genuinely collaborative, creative approach that we can make a distinctive feature of our coaching, bringing life and colour to all we do:

- the skilful art of listening and making unhurried time to get to know those we coach on a human level

- creativity as a process rooted in purposive engagement and connection, a readiness to explore "what if…" and "how would it be…" possibilities, to try the untried, and a commitment to being our very best in the moment

- an openness and excitement in shared creations and in learning together, unique explorations with each person rather than repeating the formulas that we think work best

- a selfless generosity and belief in those we coach that puts them centre stage.

7

Motivation and the paradoxes of inner drives

"I'd really want to pay attention to who's driving the bus here."

Pete Carroll on being asked what to say to a parent whose young athlete seems to have lost interest[41]

N OW, THERE IS something ironic about this chapter. I am sat at my laptop, feeling I really *ought* to write a chapter on motivation – a key theme much talked and written about in sports coaching and of course, you would think, highly relevant to confidence-centred coaching.

And yet…

It's sunny outside and I'm watching the clock slowly tick down to when I am due to meet a friend for a long swim in the sea. I'm not really feeling much drive or will to write. Although I have lots of ideas in my head, doubts seep in about whether I can bring them together in a coherent and meaningful way. And the inhibiting weight of those heavy words "ought", "should" isn't making it any easier.

---

[41] M. Gervais, *Podcast 194: Pete Carroll on the art of coaching (live)* Finding Mastery (2019). Available from https://findingmastery.com/podcasts/pete-carroll-live/ [accessed 27 September 2024].

So we have what might appear to be a classic case of lack of motivation:

- feeling disconnected from all the good reasons for writing the chapter, low on willpower and distracted by other things I could be doing

- doubting my ability to pull it off

- a wearisome judgemental sense of "should", as opposed to an energizing absorption and excitement.

But is what I feel really a lack of motivation? In fact I have a lot of motivation – to get down to the beach, meet up with my friend and enjoy the full-on sensations of swimming in a cold sea (which people tell me calls for heaps of motivation!). It's just not motivation for the focused effort, the discipline and serious concentration needed right now to bring together and capture my ideas.

In this chapter we will:

- start with an apparently simple, yet sometimes very challenging question of whose motivation we are really concerned with

- examine contrasting perspectives on how motivation is typically thought of, discussed and pressed into action

- explore some of the contradictory feelings that may be at play and look at what gets in the way

- recount another Reflective Conversation, this one with a super-active young athlete about her motivation.

The beach can wait for now.

Whose motivation?

Some years ago, whilst at Imperial College Management School and before I got into coaching, I studied and undertook research on motivation in workplace teams. A highly influential work by Psychologist Frederick Herzberg[42] opens with the question "Whose motivation are we concerned with?" This basic question – often overlooked as Herzberg went on to introduce his groundbreaking model of motivational factors – serves as a key starting point for us here.

---

[42] F. Herzberg, 'One More Time: How do you motivate employees?' in H. Clark, J. Chandler and J. Barry (eds) *Organisations and Identities* (1994).

Pretty much all the management manuals on motivation in the workplace are really coming from a place of the manager's motivation to get their people to do what they, the manager, want. In my research I called this *motivation to compliance* and distinguished it from what one would expect in the world of sports coaching where, one would think, we are more concerned with a more open *motivation for development* in our athletes. There are certainly rules to conform to and technical and tactical skills to master – but the end goal is likely to be far more about the athlete realizing their own ambition or discovering how good they can be. Or so I thought.

In practice, Herzberg's opening question seems just as relevant to the world of sports coaches – are we always genuinely driven by our athlete's ambitions and discovery of what they can do? Or do our own expectations, our sense of what counts as success and our interests and agendas creep in? A revealing test can be how we instinctively react when things go wrong, maybe a worse than anticipated result or our athlete not sticking to what we had set for them.

Here's where we come back, once again, to great coaching practice as starting from self-awareness – being able to understand and question our own motivations before jumping to address others'.

Mechanics and meaning

A second feature of motivation in management – which I see reflected in some Sports Psychology – is a rather mechanical, formulaic, inputs and outputs approach. Follow the particular prescription and motivation will result.

Back to Herzberg, and part of his pioneering approach was to shine a spotlight on how work is experienced as meaningful, instead of the inputs and outputs models of the time (which are still dominant). This led him to set out how jobs could be re-designed in such a way as to engender a sense of responsibility and accountability – opportunities for learning and growth and other job-enriching experiences – as opposed to thinking that motivation could ever be sustainable through providing (or holding back) rewards. In my own research on work teams, I saw the meaningfulness of work as critical – meaningfulness coming from a sense of purpose and knowing how one's contribution fits in. All of which directed me to want to find out about and understand the lived experience of those in work, rather than reaching for a textbook formula of how they might be brought round to fulfil someone else's agenda.

In the sports coaching world, too often we see the coach or Sports Psychologist positioned as having a ready-made formula – what to tell the athlete to do or to think. As we will see, some of the approaches, well researched and evidence-based in their own terms, point to interesting factors to consider. But the positioning feels loaded: motivation as something to be managed and cajoled in others who, if they fall short in demonstrating what is expected, have failed to apply themselves sufficiently.

We end up questioning the whole idea of motivation as a thing that people have or don't have if we come from a place of recognizing that:

- the motivations we have are certain to be different to those of the people we coach

- the focus of motivation can shift (in my case, from the concentrated, single-minded effort of writing to the pleasure of losing myself in the rhythm of a sea swim)

- between inputs and outputs lies a whole depth of meaningful emotion and feeling.

Much of what gets talked and written about motivation in sports treats it as if it were a given, quantifiable element which our athletes have more or less of. We admire the athletes who say they're really "up for it" or a team "wanting it more" – the desire to win or succeed as a measure of how much motivation they supposedly have. Or we'll refer to a particular manager or trainer as a great motivator, picturing them as if passing something almost tangible over to their charges. You'll see the question routinely asked: "How motivated are you to do…" whatever it might be "…on a scale of 1–10?"

Added to that, a distinction is also often made between so-called intrinsic and extrinsic motivation – how much am I being driven to do something by my own inner motives as opposed to satisfying the desire for some external reward (a winner's medal, prize money, others' acclamation)? On this sliding scale of motivation, the assumption is that having more of the intrinsic, inner motivation is better for sustainable action. That's obviously true, yet it carries the implication that we're talking about something people have in varying quantities, and the more they have of it, the better (so long as it aligns with those things we think they should be motivated to do).

The theory and practice of self-determination

The standard textbook model of motivation is Deci and Ryan's Self-Determination Theory[43]. This starts from an assertion that the more intrinsic motivation, the better. The emphasis, quite rightly, is on the fundamental importance of athlete-led activity. Self-Determination Theory then goes on to identify three basic conditions said to help generate such inner motivation:

- *autonomy*: as in feeling in control and able to determine what happens (where the self-determination comes from)

- *competence*: as in feeling capable of doing the task ahead

- *relatedness*: as in feeling connected and identifying with others.

Each of these opens up interesting insights into how someone may be apparently lacking that all-important inner drive and what might be done. Going back to this chapter's opening observations, I might think about the following: Why is it I don't feel in control of the writing? After all, no one is stopping me and it is clearly in my own hands. Why those creeping self-doubts, despite knowing I have tried and tested ideas to share? And why the feeling of struggling on my own, even though I know there are others to turn to for support? But if only... If I could just summon the energy to address each of these.

And here I feel something is missing in the step from identifying conditions for motivation to its supposed remedy. I see this in some coaching workshops or courses when the Self-Determination Theory model is introduced. Typically we are told these are the conditions for motivation to happen and then directed to come up with solutions, things for our low-in-motivation athlete to do or tell themselves.

So what's the problem? Surely having in mind the degree to which someone feels in control, capable and connected can only be helpful? To an extent, yes. However, even with such great intentions, the approach essentially still puts the coach in the position of judging what is enough of the "right" motivation. And it makes us the fixer when the athlete's motivation doesn't measure up to our view of the right quantity and type, rather than genuinely starting with the uniqueness of the person in front of us: what they bring,

---

[43] E. Deci and R.M. Ryan *Intrinsic Motivation and Self-Determination in Human Behavior* (2013).

what is meaningful to them and how they feel. And it is in the space between the model of motivational conditions and the supposed solutions that a whole living, complicated and deep world of meaning lies. Once again we are left with a well-researched, entirely credible but lifeless process devoid of its living subject.

The following model, I've found, takes me closer to understanding what may be going on for someone, directing me to what they actually feel and what a particular challenge means to them, and acknowledging that we can shift from one focal point or type of motivation to another.

Zigzagging with Reversal Theory

In his book *Zigzag*[44], Professor Michael Apter sets out Reversal Theory. He starts from the premise that motivation is not a fixed thing that we have more or less of – but rather we reverse back and forward, shifting between different emotions or motivational states, depending on a mix of inner feelings and thoughts and external events and environments.

From his extensive research, Professor Apter identified four pairs of seemingly contradictory motivational states that we switch or zigzag between:

• serious and playful

• conforming and rebellious

• mastery and sympathy

• self-orientated and other-orientated.

Thinking of how these might apply in a sportsperson we are coaching, the drive for *mastery* – a single-minded determination to be in control and on top of everything – might come into its own in taking on a big challenge or competition. According to Professor Apter, paradoxically this quest for mastery may at the same time veer the athlete to its opposite, to seeking out *sympathy*: maybe to be held by others or simply kinder to themselves rather than always out there at the edge. Or someone might be driven by a *serious*, studiously planned and methodical focus, caught up in analysing and performing to precise times and intensity of efforts,

---

[44] M.J. Apter *Zigzag: Reversal and paradox in human personality* (2018).

whilst simultaneously feeling the lure of a *playful*, fun or risky thrill-seeking release.

There are two key ideas in Professor Apter's model that I think are illuminating for us in coaching. The first is what he calls *protective frames*.

Protective frames

Whereas Self-Determination Theory seems to direct us to a rather top-down, prescriptive approach to increasing the amount of the "right" kind of motivation, the idea of protective frames leads us to think about the switch from one emotional or motivational state to another, without measuring if anyone thinks it is enough.

Professor Apter gives several examples of risk taking, such as driving too fast or swimming in big waves. It is as if we are caught in a *playful* bubble, enjoying ourselves and lost in the moment as if believing ourselves to be cut off from the possible consequences of our actions. When these (delusional) protective frames dissolve – maybe a sudden realization that we are not in control of the car or the next towering wave – we suddenly become vulnerable and veer to the *serious* motivational state. Slow down! Get closer to the shore!

The shifts can work the other way. Professor Apter interviewed over 60 parachutists, mapping out the switch from high anxiety (typically just before making their jump) to intense excitement (most often just after the parachute opened). In the moment of the parachute opening a protective frame literally bursts open that allows a switch from a profoundly serious, heightened awareness of the dangers to a playful, utterly euphoric exhilaration.

So bringing this back to a coaching context, we might ask how we can create a protective frame for someone undertaking their big challenge, maybe to move from an anxious, overwhelmed awareness of all the reasons why they can't do something to having a more energized excitement to try. Hold that thought.

Paradox

A second insightful idea in the Reversal Theory model is the notion of our motivations and emotions having a paradoxical quality: that in the very moment of being immersed in a certain motivational state, I can also feel the draw of its opposite. Thinking of the young people I have coached and talked with about what their motivation *feels like* (rather than the more-intrinsic-is-better loaded questions of "How motivated are you?" and "Where does your motivation come from?"), I see some of the following contradictory emotions at play:

- wanting to be independent, autonomous and treated as who they are whilst also wanting to sit in the comfort of being told what to do

- hoping to discover who they uniquely are, what interests and excites each of them personally whilst being scared of standing out from the group

- relishing being pushed hard and stretched to see how good they can be whilst also just wanting some relaxing fun

- being competitive and excited about the prospect of doing well whilst also fearful of failure and all too ready to judge themselves as "not good enough" to try.

So back to the idea of protective frames – we might first alert ourselves to the fact that what the person in front of us is feeling is always likely to be complex and contradictory, and they may not be able to articulate it for themselves. Making the unhurried time and space to ask "What else?" may help, even though the answers are unlikely to be immediately forthcoming. And from there we can start to create the safe, non-judgemental spaces in which someone battling with such contradictory emotions and feelings can be at ease and trust themselves to discover how good they can be.

Again, though, before moving to the question of what would be helpful, there is more to do in understanding the mix of emotions someone may be feeling. For this I think it helps to focus on those feelings of disconnect and doubt that get in the way and only then start to get a sense of what might help.

What gets in the way

At the risk of oversimplifying or generalizing, I see at least three typical emotions and thoughts that colour how many people approach a challenge – at sea with the contradictory emotions of desperately wanting to master something but struggling with ingrained, instinctive reactions that get in the way of finding out what they can do.

Out of place

The first picks up on one of the key conditions of motivation in the Self-Determination model: relatedness or belonging. Let's delve a little deeper into what that can feel like.

A very typical thing one hears is of someone feeling out of place. Picture the nervous newcomer to swimming – much like Jo in our earlier Reflective Conversation – feeling they don't belong in a lane (or even the same pool) as the "real" swimmers plough up and down or languidly loiter at the end of the lane. There's something so powerfully disempowering about that sense of not belonging in the space – of defining oneself as not a "proper" swimmer or runner or whatever the sport is.

I am reminded of a conversation with Kat about her journey into extreme ultra running. It all started with her feeling intimidated by what she believed to be "real" runners – the way they dressed, and bantered about times and races amongst themselves before a 5km parkrun. In her case that sense of not belonging (despite loving running) acted as a spur to find a place where she didn't feel judged for her lack of speed or "seriousness" – around 100 miles long!

But what a high cost is paid by so many other people feeling intimidated and out of place, inhibited from trying the very thing they yearn to do.

So what can a mindful, attentive coach do to help? We go back to the very basics of connection explored in Chapter 4 – how we create unhurried, non-judgemental, welcoming places.

Out of luck

Another very typical set of feelings that we have referred to before is a sense that, no matter what they do, the person in front of us feels they will fail. "I'll be your biggest challenge." "I'm never going to be fast/any good at…" And as our session gets underway they might berate themselves for not immediately getting a new technique at the first attempt. "Why can't I do this?" "I'm no good." It's as if they have a script that reads no matter how hard they try, nor how good a coach I might be, the odds are stacked against them.

And yet – back to the paradoxical, contrary emotions – at the same time I often see such a deep and meaningful desire to succeed, without necessarily a defined sense of what that might look like, other than claiming their right to a more active, fulfilling life.

Going back to our examples from swimming, in my experience two things seem to help. First is showing my belief in what they can do – so I might typically and very genuinely say that there's a swimmer in them waiting to come out (I passionately believe there's a swimmer in all of us). And second, we go back to Carol Dweck's notion of growth and fixed mindsets, emphasizing that we are trying something new, to be learnt with a patient persistence – and that it will come.

Out of time

And a third typical set of feelings that get in the way, on the face of it, may appear simply to be all about harsh realities and obvious practicalities – though sometimes digging a little deeper can reveal an unsatisfied quest for something better.

Typically one hears a resigned "I just don't have the time." "I'd love to… but how can I fit anything else in?" Here's where the notion of paradoxically contrary emotions and motivations may help us understand these feelings and begin to move to ways of helping. For sure there is an element of the painful, practical reality of living under constant pressure and endless commitments. Yet the sense I sometimes get is of being trapped in a presumption that others' needs must always come first. Any desires and dreams are a poor second best.

I think of what Michael Apter would call the conforming emotional state – a desire to fit in with what's expected and put others first; a self-subversive internal list of things we "should" do or be; to not stand out and be different. "Keep calm and carry on." (I sometimes feel the phrase is loaded with a belittling "Don't make a fuss" message.)

If so, the Reversal Theory model would tell us that lurking not far from the surface is a desire for rebelliousness, for breaking out and asserting ourselves – potentially liberating, though also possibly in ways that may actually be harmful to ourselves or others. How can we help those who feel lost in a thick fog of commitments and obligations? Perhaps it's obvious, but it's worth saying that the traditional way of coaching – by providing programmes and schedules, with little thought as to how everything else in someone's life is meant to fit in – won't work. Off the shelf, one size fits all programmes, if anything, are likely to compound the feeling of yet another thing to conform to. As stated at the start of the book, everything has to begin with the uniqueness of the person in front of us and a deep respect for their ambitions.

Reframing the question

So, in effect we have reframed the question of how to engender more motivation, as if it were a fixed, quantifiable thing, to the more complex, richer and meaning-filled question of what it feels like and what is going on. Our interest, as always, is first and foremost in how it feels – for ourselves and for our athlete. From there we can think about how to create a protective frame for someone to move from a complex, contradictory mix of emotions that can get in the way of them making the first steps toward an energizing excitement to discover just how great they can be.

What would a confidence-centred coaching approach to motivation look like, then, rooted in self-awareness, empathy and a deep, respectful curiosity to understand what someone feels – rather than jumping straight in with ready-made fix-its?

Pulling together some of the strands in this chapter, key features include:

- a readiness to put aside our own assumptions and agendas, and to understand the meaningful reality for the person in front of us

- a patient, stilling acceptance of the likely contradictoriness and mix of emotions, always grounded in holding their ambitions and aspirations in the highest regard

- a generosity with our time and interest in such a way that those we coach can be kinder to themselves, able to arrive at what really drives them and find their element.

And at this point, enough of writing – I'm off to the beach for that long-awaited swim in the sea, excited by the idea of losing and finding myself in the rhythm of swimming, of feeling at one in the water, being immersed in nature and sharing the moment with a friend.

Reflective Conversation: Pink socks with a super-active young woman

I had a long conversation with a very active 15-year-old young woman. I was curious to know what kept her involved and engaged in sports and other activities, exploring what is happening for her.

J is a member of the triathlon club where I was Head Coach. She's also a member of the local running club and youth cycling team. Through her school she competes in volleyball, hockey, cross-country, athletics... and pretty much any other sport going. And she attends ballet classes. So about as active as anyone could be.

In the course of our conversation she highlighted three things that are important for her:

- the social side – hanging out and being at ease with friends who share the same interests

- the sense of doing well and getting better at what she does

- enjoying herself and having fun.

Interestingly she went on to refer to the encouragement of her parents through them signing her up and coming to events. And her parents also came up later in talking about her being nervous before competitions – as an outlet for her to rant at! This makes me think that in young people there can be an important "me and others as a unit" element of motivation that perhaps we tend to neglect in assuming it is all about the inner drives of an independent individual. It's worth noting that the sliding scale of intrinsic/extrinsic motivation mentioned above doesn't get hold of the possible richness of such interactive support – so long as it is the young person, not the parents, "driving the bus".

The mix in the moment

Talking through her mix of emotions when racing revealed something of the paradoxical nature of her feelings. She started with a very firm "I really like competing" and yet went straight into describing at length the uncomfortable feelings of being nervous, of being intimidated by people who she instinctively assumes are better (sometimes being thrown by their fancy kit or the mind games that go on). Athletics competitions in front of a big audience further heighten her nervous sense of everyone watching, leading her to think about everything that can go wrong.

As an event then gets underway, she said she first switches to a sense of relief as she just focuses on the moment and then excitement at surprising herself as those in fancy kit fade into the background. The seemingly invincible competitor in expensive, calf-length pink compression socks is soon behind, to her delight and that of her cheering friends. The attention of the larger crowds also fades away from consciousness.

J also talked about her feelings after events – the satisfaction and sense of achievement. Interestingly, at no point did she refer to competitive positions or winning in this context. It was all about the feelings of having accomplished something, of tiredness and aching muscles together with being relaxed – as if all energy spent – and holding in mind how it felt to be running (or whatever she was doing) in that moment. For her, triathlon has the great attraction of packing three sets of experiences into one event.

Assuredness

One final aspect from a very full and open conversation is worth mentioning here. I was curious to know what she thought of friends or school peers who don't share the same active lifestyle and set of interests. Why did she think they might have dropped away whilst she maintains her interests? From her puzzled look back, the sense I took was that she couldn't comprehend any other way of being herself and so had no reason to understand or compare herself to others.

Take that in for a moment. What unassuming self-assuredness. Wouldn't you feel privileged to work with and be alongside such an athlete, of any age or ability and in whatever endeavour they set for themselves? And resolutely determined to ensure your coaching didn't get in the way of them feeling at ease with themselves, in the right place and ready to find themselves at their very best?

In summary, several things struck me from our conversation to hold on to and that help us recast our understanding of motivation:

- her easiness, satisfaction and sense of completeness at doing what she really enjoys, being in her element in the active moment, rather than only the end result

- the sense of excitement at being at her edge and further improving, even when under pressure and battling with nerves, the very contradictory mix of emotions being a part of the buzz

- how her active lifestyle connected her with others sharing similar interests

- above all, what a super example of the complexities, contradictoriness and meaning-filled beauty of what motivation can look and feel like for us to take into the next chapter, where things get significantly harder.

8
Resilience at the outer edges

"Naturally, we are amazed by those who are resilient, yet as we have focused on How do they do it? we have forgotten to also ask How does it feel?"

Meg Jay[45]

NOW, PREPARE YOURSELF.

A chapter on resilience is always going to be one of the most challenging to delve into (and for me to write). The subject matter is, by its very nature, hard and emotive: about those we coach – and perhaps ourselves too – somehow persevering against all odds; overcoming seemingly overwhelming challenges; succeeding where failure seems inevitable. It is tough and raw. And by definition it is awe-inspiring and beyond understanding. When we look for what that *somehow* is, it eludes us: "How on earth did they do that?" "Unbelievable!"

We will:

- start by stepping outside the world of sport for insights into resilience, finding something more complex and uncertain than how we typically think of it as about the exceptional, as all about strength and determination

---

[45] M. Jay *Supernormal: Childhood adversity and the untold story of resilience* (2017).

- catch up with Dr Kat Ganly as she tells us about two further monumental ultra challenges and shares some lessons along the way

- think about what we can do, as coaches, to help those at the outer edges of what seems possible

- close with another Reflective Conversation, with further insights into being with those literally on the edge.

Perhaps because of their heroic, inexplicable quality, there is a fascination with those amazing sportspeople, intrepid adventurers and other motivational speakers who have undertaken extraordinary challenges or faced life-changing experiences and gone on to tell their stories. Certainly there are women and men who have faced hard to imagine challenges and somehow found a way through. They stand out as examples of resilience personified: a steely determination; a single-minded commitment to getting through; the embodiment of endurance. And indeed that is a part of their remarkable tales. But I wonder. Aside from the awe they inspire, what do we really understand and learn from such daring, defeat-defying stories?

In this chapter we will look at resilience in a quite distinctive, narrow context: when those we coach reach a point where they just don't know how to carry on, at their outer limits and yet, somehow, go beyond them. In this respect, so-called grit, strength and determination, bouncing back from setbacks, impressive though they all are, belong somewhere else. Here we are seeking to be with those facing in the moment battles with their deepest uncertainties, beyond what they believe is possible. The outer frontier of confidence-centred coaching, at the far reaches and most daunting features of our new landscape.

Lessons from childhood adversity

When we hear of young people who have overcome traumatic childhood experiences and yet gone on to live seemingly successful, fulfilling lives, we instinctively wonder about what special qualities they had. How was it that they didn't sink further into a life of continuing limited opportunities, of perpetuating patterns of harm or hardship?

Early research in this field set out to uncover these exceptional, rare qualities – only to find in study after study that overcoming adversity and trauma was far more common than had been supposed and that this ability to get through was not limited to a few unusually gifted people. One of the leading researchers and writers on resilience, Ann Masten, entitled her book *Ordinary Magic*[46]. As she summarizes, whilst a few exceptional cases exist of children overcoming heavy odds because of extraordinary talents, resilience is common and typically arises from what she called ordinary human resources and basic – seemingly obvious – protections such as close relationships with competent and caring adults and a belief in life having meaning and purpose.

Another key finding is highlighted by the quote from Meg Jay above. In her book *Supernormal* she recounts stories of people she has seen in her therapeutic practice who grew up in very disturbing, chaotic or disruptive circumstances: victims of sexual abuse, children of addicted parents, survivors of commonplace violence and more. The power of these stories lies in how she brings to light and recounts the feelings experienced. And with each story the question of how they went on to succeed – the "How do they do it?" – seems to slip away, as if missing the point. The path to so-called success is rarely clearly seen and almost never truly felt as a triumphant escape from the past.

We tend to think of resilience as all about single-mindedness. This certainly can have its place but, for those living with past or present trauma, Meg Jay and other researchers show it typically sits alongside a whole mix of seemingly contradictory emotions: a sense of weakness, vulnerability, being out of control. In another classic study, Boris Cyrulnik[47] uses the term *oxymoron* to capture something of this contradictoriness he found in the most harrowing of life stories of what he called his "wounded victors": young survivors of concentration camps, child soldiers, trafficked children and more.

"A child who has survived an extreme situation is shaped like an oxymoron: their guilt is innocent, their pride shameful and their heroism is cowardly; they were found guilty in their age of innocence; they are ashamed because they are proud of having survived when the people they loved did not make it; and their heroism proves to them

---

[46] A. Masten *Ordinary Magic: Resilience in development* (2015).

[47] B. Cyrulnik *Resilience: How your inner strength can set you free from your past* (2009).

that they were a coward because, had they really been brave, they would have died along with their family." (gender pronouns changed)

Boris Cyrulnik.

I said it was emotional.

An obvious point is that of course we can't assume that an apparent ability to absorb and deal with pressure or hardship is really what is felt – or that those who come through difficulties will have the same sense of unscathed victory as an onlooker might suppose. The stories reveal that, whilst they try to draw on a courage and determination to keep going, there can also be a deep uncertainty and doubting. And triumphs and conquests may feel hollow if they come from the darkest of places.

I know from my own childhood experience that when difficult things happen, there can be a numbing sense of confusion and guilt. If it could be put into words (the fact that it can't being a key point) it might be "I must have done something bad for these bad things to have happened. But I don't know what. Or why." The understanding, ability to articulate what was felt and self-compassion not to blame yourself come much, much later. In the meantime we carry on. What else is there to do? A child trapped in their confusing, uncaring world is unable to conceive of the possibility that life doesn't have to be that way, that what they take to be "normal" is anything but, and that how they respond is, as Meg Jay says, supernormal.

Of course when we turn to resilience in an athlete's performance there is a vital difference: they are there by choice. No child chooses their circumstances. Nor are tragic events that might occur in later life and shake the very foundations of our being something that we have opted for. Even looking at childhood adversity and trauma for lessons for athletic endeavours and coaching, I know, carries a risk of seeming to trivialize the heartrending experiences many endure, in whatever form or stage in life, through no fault of their own. We'll come back to this key difference between resilience in a place that is *unintended* as opposed to *intended*.

A second key difference is of course the time-limited nature of what is experienced. In the narrow sense I suggest we look at resilience in athletic endeavours, it is only for a finite time – though in that moment the feeling typically is that there is no end to it. Childhood adversity, however, is relentlessly present, day after day, year after year. Even one-off traumatic events in early years will continue to impact and shape a young person's reality long after their initial occurrence. In contrast, even the harshest of athletic experiences rarely leave such long-lasting imprints.

As we will see, though, in our narrow sports context, there is something of the contradictoriness, vulnerability and inability to conceive of any other way that is relevant to resilience in the most testing of moments.

Let's take a break and go for a run.

Of dragons and Greek legends

Back in Chapter 5 we left Dr Kat Ganly as she ran on ahead and we paused to take in what she had said about letting go of fear of failure and finding herself running with a fluency, sense of control and excitement to see where it would take her. With what she described as the best race of her life – the 145-mile Grand Union Canal ultra – now behind her, the Welsh mountains are again looming after her earlier, unsuccessful attempt. And beyond them lies the most prestigious and hardest ultra: the Spartathlon.

Back to face the Dragon

Two years on from her first attempt at the notorious Dragon's Back, Kat returned – this time with her amazing success at the Grand Union Canal, her newfound ability to run without fearing the worst and a new excitement about where her running could take her.

The Dragon's Back takes place over five days, running over 300km from North to South along Wales' highest ridges and mountains with fairly minimal safety cover or marshalling. For Kat there was an added challenge that she is scared of heights. Day 1 includes scaling and running along Crib Goch – a terrifying knife-edge ridge with sheer drops either side. A few weeks before, Kat had travelled to Snowdonia to check out this segment. On the first day of the reconnaissance trip the route was shrouded in mist and so relatively benign as the sheer drops either side could not be seen. But the next day the sun came out to reveal it in all its frightening, stomach-churning clear detail. Kat found herself so scared that she was unable to keep going and turned back without going any further. So, as she says, not the best confidence-boosting preparation.

Come race day and over 25 miles into the running, conditions were wet and grey as Kat approached the turning for the ascent to Crib Goch. Much to her dismay the marshals directed the runners up onto the ridge, rather than along the safer, lower-level bad weather route. She began running up, dreading what was to come.

By chance another runner was just behind her who seemed even more terrified than her. She laughingly recounts that at first his wailing was a little off-putting, but she felt compelled to reassure him – and maybe in the process distracted herself from her own fears. Somehow she talked herself and her companion through it and together they made it over the worst of the Dragon's Back.

On Day 3 Kat met two other women running at a similar pace and they decided to run together all the way to the end, helping each other with the tricky navigation and through various incidents along the way. She says their support helped carry her through Day 4, which she started and ended in tears. "Day 3 we all worked well together, they definitely dragged me through Day 4… and were really propping me up." Kat says she might have run faster on the last day as she was so excited to finish, but was more than happy to complete the event with her companions without whom she would have been slower overall. She had tamed the Dragon.

The stuff of legends

Back on her feet working in A&E the very next day there was no time for rest or basking in any glory (not that ultra runners seem to do much of that at the best of times). Looming ahead was another major challenge which Kat says she had been trying to ignore – having been selected for the Great Britain team undertaking the legendary Spartathlon, where long-distance running began. The Spartathlon follows Pheidippides' steps from Athens to Sparta, 250km in 36 hours. Along the way are very tight cut-off times beyond any of Kat's previous best times.

Acutely aware of the pressure, she was persuaded to get an experienced coach. Kat says that initially she was very hesitant about having one – something she thought was for "proper" runners, not someone like her (despite her amazing achievements and GB selection). That feeling of being out of place amongst "real" athletes — which we saw in Chapter 5 when we introduced our Four Ps and in the last chapter on what gets in the way — was also present in how she described joining the GB team. She said they were all very friendly and impressive — "and then there was me".

Kat says from the start she went off too fast but felt really happy running at her speed. The first marathon had a cut-off time of four and a half hours, which she sailed through with more than 30 minutes to spare. Next cut-off: 50 miles to be done in under a frightening 9 hours (with Kat's PB up to that point 9:17). She went through in a staggering 8 hours! At 100 miles she was still running way beyond herself, picking up a new 100-mile PB of 19 hours. She felt lifted by the support along the route, especially from local children who had been given the day off school to cheer the legend-chasing runners.

Being in a place of pain

And then, as she described it, "Everything went wrong." On the long sections of road running she developed extremely painful thigh muscles, no doubt also due to the amazing speed she'd kept up until then. She described the last 15km as so painful that she reached the point of thinking she would drop out. She had been running at her strong pace for almost 24 hours, but over that last hour had been sick several times, was in real pain, and felt cold and utterly beaten.

She stopped at an aid station just before dawn, slumped in a chair and despaired of being able to get up and go on. Her partner, who had been supporting her at each point, was unsure what to say or how to help, seeing her in such a bad way. One of the GB crew members, however, said to her in a matter of fact, dispassionate way that the sun would be up in a few minutes, so "Get on with it."

For around five minutes she struggled to walk, telling herself the crew member was wrong. How could she even take one step?! Then gradually she got back to something resembling moving forward and started to feel a little better — though still struggling and convinced she couldn't do it. Remember: resilience is not always about steely, single-minded determination — in the most testing of moments, it's vulnerability and a kind of muddling through despite what we think we can do.

At this point in her story Kat also stops to give us a strong reality check. She says it would be nice to think there are things one can say to oneself or other strategies that would somehow block out or take you above the pain. Kat's view from her experience is that "You don't get through such pain" as if it can be cleverly put to one side or stubbornly ignored. She tells us that you have to accept that in an ultra, there are large portions where you will be really hurting. All over. And there is nothing you can do. "If you want to finish you have to accept it."

She is still unsure how she made those last miles as her quads had stopped working. By that stage even walking felt beyond her. Reliving the experience she laughs that a photo of her approaching the finish line makes it look as if she is running with a commendable, forward-leaning style. In fact she was close to toppling over with little or no control of her legs.

What we learn at the feet of Pheidippides

As she pays due homage at the statue of Pheidippides (tradition dictates each runner must kiss his feet), with a laurel garland and a look of bewildered astonishment that she made it through, we can pause to dwell on what we have witnessed and what lessons we can draw.

First, my sense from Kat's amazing story and my own experience of working with other ordinary-extraordinary endurance athletes is that people do get through such extremes – much in the same way as the ordinariness of surviving childhood adversity and trauma. And at its heart is a *mystery*: we just don't know, and in one sense trying to find a single factor, formula or set of tips belittles their awe-inspiring, beyond belief achievement precisely because it comes from a place of such mixed emotions and vulnerability.

And here's the thing. Too often we rush to find a way of explaining or categorizing an experience, to find the words for what we have witnessed – and miss out on the chance simply to take in the wonder and inexplicable magic of what has happened. When I think of my own experiences of being out at those far edges, beyond what I felt I could do, the memories come back with a humility and gratitude – "How lucky am I!" I don't know how I did it, but wow – am I grateful for having done so.

Some elements that seem to be common, though, are first a depth of willpower – or what Kat calls her stubbornness. Yet as we have seen this sits alongside deep self-doubts. Think of Kat's description of being out of place in the company of "proper" athletes or being unworthy of a coach. And I think of the moments I have felt at my absolute limit and beyond it – a desperation to get to the end, not knowing how to keep going and yet, like a child in a confusing world, unable to grasp that there might be an option to stop.

A second element is the acknowledgement and acceptance of extreme discomfort and pain – as Kat put it, "You don't get through it. It's just crap." Yet we are surrounded by the opposite messages: "When the going gets tough, the tough get going", our so-called "grit" and how we respond under pressure as somehow revealing our true worth (it doesn't, our values and how we show up for others do); and most infamously Lance Armstrong's "Pain is temporary, pride is forever" (with help from EPO as it turned out). I know in the past I fell into the trap of berating myself as things got really hard, shouting at myself to "just get on with it". After all, I was told as a child: "Stop making a fuss."

I now think this kind of bludgeoning ourselves can too easily make it even harder than it already is. It tells us to ignore what we know we are feeling and takes us to an all or nothing, get through it or fail way of thinking. For some, maybe it works. For me and those I coach I have found a more helpful way of thinking is to acknowledge when things are really hard and then re-locate ourselves within the experience.

This might be by reminding ourselves of the purpose and meaningfulness, the why; it might be reclaiming the place as properly ours, "How brilliant to be here", our living masterpiece in the making, right here right now; or shifting focus to the narrow space immediately ahead, one step, one stroke at a time; or the reaffirmation of who we are, the "This is hard – and I do hard things" self-talk in our Four Ps. But again, we are beyond clever tips and tricks or things to say – much of this happens in an instinctive, intuitive place with the words following behind.

Thirdly, an interesting theme running through both sets of stories from Kat, here and in Chapter 5, is the significance of the people around her. I'm struck by the effect that quiet, unpressured encouragement can have in the darkest moments of doubt: her partner's calm, easy-going "Why not give it a go?" on the morning of the Grand Union Canal ultra, recounted in Chapter 5; the GB crew member's simple "Get on with it" in the bleakest minutes before dawn at the Spartathlon. And from the Dragon's Back there was the reassurance of being with others – her support when another runner was really struggling and then later her being "propped up" by her two women companions through the hardest day.

Practical guides for being there

What can we as coaches do if we are accompanying those we coach into the far outer reaches of what seems possible? Much as we have seen the athlete's own experience can feel overwhelming and beyond them, so too we are likely to become acutely aware of our own limitations – as if frozen in the moment, unsure what to do or say. I think of three kinds of action that can help guide us. They are all rooted in being present and alongside.

Keep it safe

The first takes us back to the idea of *unintended* and *intended resilience* as a key difference between those who find themselves in the most difficult, harrowing circumstances and those who choose to go to a place of pain. In the following respect, though, there is perhaps an important similarity: the need for someone external to decide whether safety comes first and take them away from harm.

A young person growing up in the kind of chaotic, confusing, threatening environment that Meg Jay and others recount has little or no conception that it doesn't have to be that way. They need the caring, competent adult that Ann Masten identifies as a protector to step in or at the very least show a different way. There are times when our duty of care to those we coach may require us to step in and save them from serious harm. It is precisely because in the moment of the athlete's intent being so strong and all-consuming – to finish at all costs, to keep going despite real dangers of harm or events spiralling out of all control – their ability to discern what is safe and what is genuinely harmful becomes clouded.

And what difficult decisions to make! So much of this happens instinctively and in the moment – so long as we are in tune with ourselves and those we coach.

Getting shouty

A second type of directive action in these extreme situations is one that might seem to run counter to all we have said about avoiding the "fixing reflex", not telling athletes what they must do and instead helping them find and attune themselves to what is right for them. In these extreme, up against it moments, though, a far more directive, what might seem even brutal approach may be called for.

Adam, one of the athletes I've been coaching long term, recently took part in a relay swim across the English Channel. He was super prepared and the team spirit was high. Shortly after they set off at 3:00am in the dark the conditions changed, very much for the worse: high winds and a big threatening, sick-inducing swell. Adam battled through his first hour-long section and was resting, readying himself for his next turn. A teammate was just five minutes into her swim and finding the conditions utterly overwhelming. She kept stopping, repeatedly looked at her watch as if it would somehow shorten the ordeal, and reverted to an ineffective breaststroke that meant she was actually making no progress at all. It was looking like the attempt would have to be abandoned.

Aware of her suffering and realizing how close they were to not making it, Adam gathered the rest of the team together on deck. For the whole of her remaining time in the turbulent sea they shouted out a count for every single stroke: "one, two, one, two, one, two…" Somehow, much to their collective credit, she made it through her hour and was even able to swim her next two, later turns. And the team made it all the way to France.

Helping take someone through their struggle by breaking things down to the most immediate of tasks and commanding them – in effect taking the thinking away from them – may be what's needed in those specific moments of utter exhaustion and clouded, despairing thinking. One stroke after another through the waves, one step at a time in an ultra run, one pedal turn after another up a long, gruelling hill countless hours into a multi-day mountain bike event. My sense, though, is that this is only effective when it comes from a place of genuine care and belief.

And back to the time-limited nature of such situations: as soon as possible we want to give back to the athlete the feeling they are in control, able to work through the hardest of challenges and draw strength from themselves, rather than others.

Stay present

How often does the opposite happen, though? Think about the typical reactions we see from managers and coaching staff when a football team is up against it: another goal let in, heads dropping, nothing seems to be going right and the opposition rampant. I wonder if, in that moment, players would be feeling something similar to the sense of hopelessness, no answers to be found, beyond their limits and not knowing how to turn things around that I know from the extremes of my endurance sports. And there at pitch side what would be going through the minds of the coaches? Rather than as soon as possible giving back control (what Sports Psychologists would call autonomy), we see frustration get the better of the coach – they tense up and become increasingly judgemental, stuck in an exasperated "Why don't they just do what I told them to?"

There is a fascinating piece of research by Rob Mason and his colleagues at Melbourne University, analysing in-game feedback by Australian Football League coaches to their players[48]. Over the course of a season of more than 20 games Rob and his colleagues captured the interactions between a team of four or five coaches and the messages sent to players as they performed.

As one might expect, when the team was winning, the feedback tended to be more positive; when losing, negative feedback was *three times* more frequent than positive. What stands out from the quote below is how much of this feedback turned to prescriptive, controlling instructions.

"Instead of simply describing performance in their feedback (e.g., 'your pressure has been down in the last 5 minutes'), coaches overwhelmingly prescribed future performance (e.g., 'you need to lift your pressure') at a rate of 4 prescriptive comments to every 1 descriptive comment."

Rob Mason

Rob goes on to highlight how controlling the coaches' feedback tended to be – 80% of messages in a losing quarter – with very few messages supporting the players, suggesting options or asking for their views. The impression given is of the thinking being taken away from the players – their views of what might be happening and what to do about it.

Interestingly, the research also revealed that the number of messages dropped significantly when the result of a game seemed pretty much inevitable –

[48] R. Mason, *Game day feedback: What happens in the AFL coaches' box*, Rob Mason (2023). Available from: https://www.masonlearning.com/blog/what-happens-in-the-afl-coaches-box [Accessed 20 September 2024].

both when the team were clearly heading for a win and faced with a loss. So, in the latter case, at the very time a team might be feeling rock bottom and unable to find a way through, the coaches seemed to be less present, their energy turned elsewhere. Rob suggests this may reflect a sense of the game slipping out of the coaches' control (we might quietly say they never had rightful control in the first place). I also wonder if there is something of distancing themselves from defeat, when this might be the very moment to be most clearly present and alongside the players.

Here, we go back to the idea of critical coaching moments from Chapter 6, as Michael Gervais identifies them: the two to three seconds after a significant action such as the athlete trying something new, or experiencing a moment of success or, as in this case, failure. In those brief few seconds a coach can have an extraordinary impact: showing faith and belief, being a steady constant alongside; or displaying a "You're on your own" dismissiveness, a defeated sense that all is lost, beyond hope, and a resigned disappointment.

Here again is another lesson I learnt from my friend Kat. When she first asked for people to run with her over sections of her 100-mile challenges, I remember thinking to myself "But what can I say? How can I be of any help?" I had no experience of covering that kind of distance. She said it would help her but I had no idea how.

It seems obvious now, but as we ran side by side through the dark and into the dawn I realized it was the *being there* that helped her most. No need for pep talks or even a speech about my Four Ps of Confidence-Centred Coaching! Remember Margo Bristow's "wisdom in the room"? Kat knew far better than I did how to put one foot in front of the other for 100 miles. All I had to do was be present, alert to her needs and allow the rest to take care of itself.

And when it's done

So we come toward the end of our extraordinary challenge. Maybe there are tears of disbelief – I know I have shed many, both as an endurance athlete somehow making it to the end and as a coach being alongside others as they are overwhelmed by the mystery and magnificence of what they have done. And this is the essence of understanding resilience and being alongside those out at the far edges:

- a humbling sense of inexplicable mystery to sit with in stillness and gratitude

- the paradox of a deep-seated determination – or stubbornness as Kat calls it – in the very moment of greatest vulnerability and self-doubt

- the quiet and beautiful power of a reassuring, positive presence.

And here's another important lesson from what we saw of resilience and childhood adversity: making space for someone to share what they *felt*, the mix of emotions, the highs and lows, the moments of despairing "I don't know if I can do this" and yet mysteriously, magically carrying on; rather than only focusing on what they *did*, the achievement of times and places, of getting through to the end, amazing though that all is. As we have seen throughout the book, whilst the traditional view of coaching is all about instructional prowess, our greatest and most impactful coaching moments might come from a place of skilful, curious, quiet listening.

On that note, I recall conversations with Kat about how uncomfortable we both can feel with expressions of adulation and awe from others – in no short supply in her case, given her achievements. These can (albeit unintentionally) be distancing. Lavish praises, though undoubtedly well earned, feel so out of tune with all the uncertain feelings and self-doubts that we experience in the very moments of what may be our greatest achievements. And incidentally, being told how "you're going to smash it" or "nail it" before a big, nerve-racking event seems likely to heighten these feelings rather than quell them.

Two further thoughts before our next Reflective Conversation. The first comes from Brené Brown. Remember those heroic, awe-inspiring exemplars of resilience we mentioned at the start of the chapter? I wonder how much more relatable and impactful for us their stories would be if they could reveal more of the vulnerability and the humble, wonder-filled mystery of coming through what they did. It might not provide a list of tips for things to do, but for certain it would help us identify with them, deepen our connections to our own inner courage and make us more than awe-struck spectators.

And secondly, I think of the *ordinariness* of resilience that we saw in the studies of childhood adversity. I believe this tells us some enormously positive and hopeful things:

- that the exceptional lies in us all

- to never underestimate what extraordinary things those who come for coaching may be capable of, given expert care and encouragement

- the humbling privilege of being able to be a part of the magical stories they create.

Reflective Conversation: On the edge with Dr Rebecca Williams

Thinking of the exceptional being in each of us, there is one activity or sport that I just cannot see myself ever being brave enough to attempt – the very thought leaves me shrinking inward with fear! I love being in the mountains, hiking or cycling, their solidity and permanence filling me with a stilling wonder. It is most definitely not the precariousness of clinging to the side of a rock face. But what better place to understand what it is to be out there, exposed and literally on an edge?

So, thinking about the narrow context of resilience we have focused on in this chapter, I was keen to have a conversation with Climbing Instructor and Consultant Psychologist Dr Rebecca Williams. Rebecca is the author of a super book, *Climb Smarter*[49]. Not something I can see myself ever putting into practice but full of ideas, lessons and stories that have parallels and common themes with those in this book.

At the rock face

When I outlined my nightmare vision of me frozen, overwhelmed by fear, clinging for dear life to a rock face, one of the first things Rebecca did was talk about the appropriateness of each challenge – as if to gently point out that it's not all cliff edge stuff! Where things can get more precarious and leave someone in that place of fearful immobility is when a climber is aiming for a grade of climb they have not reached before and, as happens, conditions change for the worse. So there is something of aiming for the right degree of challenge as well as a readiness to respond to external events beyond anyone's control.

She also talked about the mindset with which some climbers approach their particular challenge – seeing it in stark, succeed or fail terms. I instinctively think of climbing as all about getting to the summit. Yet Rebecca emphasized the importance of approaching a climb with a more open curiosity: "How far can I go? How skilfully? And how well can I reach for the next ledge or

---

[49] R. Williams *Climb Smarter: Mental skills and techniques for climbing* (2022).

bolt... then the one after?" This very much echoes how we can reframe the space we are in and redefine each challenge that we saw in our Four Ps in Chapter 5.

For some less experienced climbers the fact they are not able to see the top of their proposed climb – literally as well as in terms of picturing themselves there – is enough to make them reluctant to start. Rebecca encourages an approach of seeing what they can do – how far, with or without various equipment, with different techniques or supporting climbing partners. And much as I say about times and podium places for those I coach, reaching the top has a way of taking care of itself.

Reflecting back on this, I wonder how many of my moments of doubting if I could carry on would have been pre-empted by softening the way I saw each challenge, taking a less stark, more nuanced view of what would count as success. The very fact of seeing a challenge in succeed or fail terms must hasten the onset of those very crunch moments of feeling we are beyond our limits.

Echoing Kat's place of pain, Rebecca also talked about the acceptance of discomfort. Some climbers she has worked with seem to want the moment of heightened anxiety and stress to be over as quickly as possible. That way it may be they actually hasten themselves to the point of self-doubt, of tensing up and believing they can't go on – I picture this "I just want this to be over" as a head-on rush to inner helplessness. Rebecca talked about the calming strength from a climber being able to stay with their discomfort and that way end up stretching themselves beyond what seemed possible.

And she pointed out acceptance is not surrender – accepting the discomfort, doubt, fear is not the same as surrendering to it but "somehow allowing it to wash over you and keep moving toward not the goal as such but the meaningful or valued place".

Mastery of fear or craft?

Interestingly, and without any prompting from me, our conversation led Rebecca to pose the obvious question that is hanging there: why? Why do people keep putting themselves in terrifying positions, pitting themselves against a void? In climbing she said some of this comes from a passion for the mountains. She also sees a desire in many to attain a form of *mastery*.

In this respect Rebecca made a distinction between mastery of fear and mastery of craft. Someone might see their goal as being to overcome their fear, to wrestle with those anxious thoughts that undermine us in the very moment of greatest challenge. Yet, for Rebecca, it is in focusing on mastery of craft – skilful climbing – that the fear is unlocked. "You don't master fear." Instead she encourages her climbers to shift their attention to the small details of each moment of a climb, each next move: such as the positioning of the feet, bringing the hips into the rock – a moment to moment concentration and mindfulness that allows self-doubting thoughts and feelings to go.

On the edge

And back to my vision of me frozen in fear, petrified and unable to move. Rebecca talked through what she would do to help someone should they get themselves to such a state of inner helplessness. Just as we saw in our Practical guides for being there section, a brief intervention might be needed to break things down, to be a calm, for the moment controlling presence. She might hold eye contact; breathe in time with the scared climber; tell them to only look at the immediate place ahead, rather than all the way up the scary heights; then help them reassess the technique that they temporarily lost.

Noticeably, though, she also brought the conversation round to how best to anticipate and prepare for such situations. She designs training sessions to practise problem solving and thinking under pressure – including sometimes a measure of forced hyperventilating to then practise calming techniques to feel in control.

Will you ever find me on a rock face, roped up and ready to focus on the next move that will eventually take me to the top? Probably not, but I definitely would want Rebecca as my guide and tutor if I ever did.

Our next and final chapter turns from those we coach out on an edge to us as coaches: when we feel like we can't go on or don't know how to summon up the energy, the will and wherewithal to keep going. Some thoughts from our look at resilience to take with us include:

- a recognition that even our most well rehearsed and refined mindset strategies, such as those set out in the Four Ps in Chapter 5, can only take us so far, and that some challenges go to places far beyond what seems possible

- that in such out at the edge moments there is an unfathomable mystery of how those we coach come through, to be acknowledged in humility and wonder – like sitting silently before a masterpiece, taking in its deep impact without the need for explanations, labels or noisy praise

- at the same time, an acknowledgement of the ordinariness of resilience: that the exceptional lies in us all rather than only a few extraordinary people

- that if we are truly connected to and mindful of those we accompany into their darkest places, we will instinctively know in the moment how best to be present: when to hold back, when to step in; when to offer words of encouragement or of consolation and when to be silent – always present and believing in the extraordinary things people can do.

One final set of thoughts to lead us into the next chapter. We have as much of a duty of care and safe wellbeing to ourselves as we have to those we coach. And we might suppose that we are always required to have a steadfast, resolute level of energy and focus. In fact, it is perfectly normal to feel a mix of seemingly contradictory emotions – and, in the words of Brené Brown, in our vulnerability lies our greatest measure of courage.

9
Protecting our coaching energy

"So how are you feeling? Right now?"

THIS FINAL CHAPTER explores how we can look after and protect our energy – possibly the greatest asset we bring to our coaching. And what difficult, challenging times these last few years have been to test our resolve and energy.

In line with the theme repeated throughout the book – and highlighted in the last chapter on resilience in those we coach – we want to look beyond *what to do*. There are already many guides in this area, focused on practical actions and steps to support our wellbeing as coaches. As we have done throughout the book, we want first to delve deeper into *what is felt* – to be attuned to what is happening for us and for those we coach. In this way we arrive at truly knowing in ourselves, as if instinctively and naturally, what is right for each of us to do.

We will:

- suggest a different way of thinking about our energy, less about quantity and more about key qualities to seek out and develop

- take a stroll through a gallery of images that will help give colour and life to what is felt

- conclude with a plea for a kinder, more caring way of being, in the places we coach in, for those we coach and for ourselves

- in our last Reflective Conversation, share an insightful view of where we are.

From the outset it is worth emphasizing that if we reach a point of feeling over-stretched and undervalued, drained, with nothing more to give, then stepping back is almost certainly the best thing to do. This chapter is not about ready-made fix-its to see ourselves through, to grit our teeth and soldier on regardless. It comes from a place of self-care, of recognizing our limits and being as attentive to our own needs as we would want to be to those we coach.

The chapter draws on workshops and webinars I have run with coaches across all sports and with British Triathlon coaches. Some were in the midst of the COVID pandemic when there was a common feeling of being right up against it – successive lockdowns and then restricted openings calling for extraordinary adaptability and energy. At the time there was much talk and evidence of burnout, of coaches feeling they could not carry on giving out so much. Even at the best of times coaching requires a selfless generosity, a readiness to give out without always getting much back. How much harder it was when everything closed down, long planned for events were cancelled and reactions to all the uncertainty swung between a frantic desperation to keep going and forlorn abandonment.

In the workshops, to help us focus on our felt experience, we used lots of imagery – some of these images are shared here as illustrative examples. You are sure to have your own ways of thinking about – and knowing in yourself – the various elements of energy that we will look at. As you read this chapter, try to tap into your experiences: what images come to mind of your coaching energy, what you bring of yourself to each coaching session or contact? Imagine yourself sharing these images and feelings with others. Not a measure of high or low but something that conveys the depth and colour of how you feel as you ready yourself to coach.

And this is the thing: we tend to think of energy in a rather one-dimensional way, as all about *quantity*. We'll say someone who appears very active and positive is full of energy; or maybe we'll say we are low on energy, don't have much left, our tank's empty. From there we'll jump to the obvious remedies: eating and sleeping well, avoiding stressful situations or contacts, maybe even taking a break from all the high pressure commitments. All very sound and probably the very advice we would offer to an over-stretched, run-down athlete (but don't always follow ourselves). What's missing, it seems to me, is that the remedies are not always in touch with where we are and what we are experiencing.

Here I want to suggest a different way: of focusing on the *qualities* of our coaching energy, what it feels like and what it enables. In this way, by connecting with the feelings and the sense of what it can do, we can begin to truly know and value its essential qualities – and instinctively know how to look after them.

Think of a number...

Let's start with a brief introductory exercise I used in one of the workshops that will help us get beyond the idea of energy as all about how much or little we have.

Ask yourself: if you could put a number from 0 to 10 on how you are feeling right now, what would it be? Zero would be absolutely wrung out with no desire to do anything, and 10 would be brimming over with unstoppable energy.

Write your number down in the centre of a piece of paper.

And now draw out from it a series of lines, like a spider diagram, and jot down what you are aware of as contributing to that number. As an example, below is one I did for myself when I was preparing for one of the workshops: part of a Performance Learning Week for GB Triathlon Coaches.

I was certainly a bit nervous, wondering how the workshop would go, unsure how the participants would react to my ideas and mindful of all the technical details that needed to work (not a strong point of mine!). Maybe 7 was too high. At the same time I knew I had a great opportunity to present to a super audience and that the ideas had proved really helpful to others and to me. Hmm – maybe 8 would have been more accurate. At the same time I was feeling a bit hungry – when did I last eat? I was also feeling exhilarated from a dip in the cold sea that morning (though my feet had yet to warm up). At a deeper level I was feeling grateful for being healthy and well.

How am I feeling?

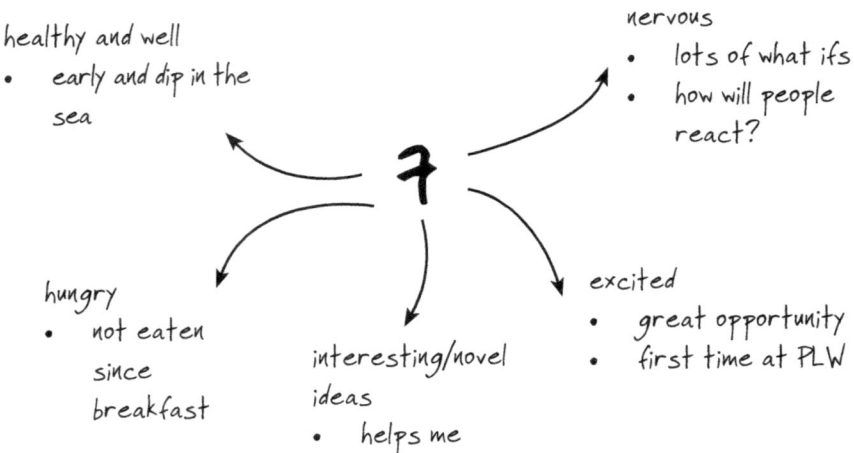

healthy and well
- early and dip in the sea

nervous
- lots of what ifs
- how will people react?

hungry
- not eaten since breakfast

interesting/novel ideas
- helps me

excited
- great opportunity
- first time at PLW

What kind of mix of feelings and factors have you identified?

Before moving on from your spider diagram, imagine you are suddenly asked to go and coach a session – right now. One of the other coaches is unwell and you are needed, ready or not. Think of the complex mix of all that is going on for you that, whether front of mind or more in the background, you will be taking to the session. Hold that thought.

Perhaps it's an obvious point but note that our gauge of energy reserves to draw on goes up and down as we turn our focus to the breadth and depth of what is going on for us. This is not to suggest that we simply make ourselves feel better by shifting our focus to positives – that might have a short-term effect, but we want something deeper and more sustainable.

And there is something important in the flux and fluidity of what we might be feeling that the language of energy as a quantity does not lend itself to. As coaches we can too easily believe that we have to be on a full-on setting, transmitting high energy all the time. The danger is that we keep giving out until it feels like we have nothing more to give – a kind of all or nothing that doesn't allow for the type of complexities and mixed feelings we might have. We come to resent the amount of time spent seemingly for others' benefit and how it eats into the rest of our lives. The lack of appreciation gnaws away. A sense of isolation, "Why bother?" and burnout beckons.

Qualities of coaching energy

So what are these energy-affirming qualities? For me, there are three.

An **enthusiasm** *that enables engagement*

Remember how we thought of an excitement in our coaching, of not knowing what will happen and having a thrilled anticipation about what lies ahead? If I can bring that kind of open, inquisitive enthusiasm to a coaching session, it will generate an engagement from those I'm coaching. Their focus and readiness to go with what we're working on will, in turn, lift me and help me lose myself in the flow of the coaching. The creation of a shared energy that leaves us all wondering where the time went and keen to come back for more.

And as we've said before, there is nothing of a "fake it till you make it" pretence. For sure there are times when I consciously have to summon up an enthusiasm from within. As we saw in Chapter 3: Confident coaches, focusing on the purpose, translating this into an adaptable, clearly focused plan and thinking of how I want to be present can all help. Most importantly, it comes from a place of being genuine and true to myself: knowing what I really value, what I can offer and fundamentally believing in what others can do given the right encouragement and expert care.

An **attentive focus** *that enables spontaneous creativity*

There is also a quality of coaching energy that is more about a concentrated, purposeful effort to focus on the person or group of people in front of us. Where they are at and what will help them most. Think of Stephen Rollnick's calm, compassionate, curious attentiveness that we highlighted at the start of the book as one of the coach's greatest skills. And that in turn seems to free us up to be creative, to try out unplanned ideas that come in the moments of connection, to respond openly and go with whatever those we are coaching come up with, no matter how unexpected or odd that might at first seem.

A **wholeheartedness** *that enables us to find the best in ourselves and others*

Brené Brown's definition of wholehearted living is "engaging in our lives from a place of worthiness[50]." In terms of coaching, this means showing up as I

---

[50] B. Brown *The Gifts of Imperfection* (2022).

am, committed to giving the best I can, imperfections and all. I want to draw on a quality of energy that comes from who I am and want to be. There's an authenticity that others respond to, as if invited to be themselves too.

Wholeheartedness also has an element of risk: of taking a plunge and putting ourselves out there, knowing we don't have all the answers and, in truth, have little idea what may happen, how others will respond or what the end result might be. My energy needs to have a quality of being unassuming yet self-assured, a relaxed alertness, being ready to respond to whatever may happen, with ego and pride put aside, whilst knowing my "worthiness" is not in question.

So we are a long, long way from the realm of whipped up, frothy on the surface hyperactive energy. We are drawing on something far deeper, personally meaningful and sustainable.

A gallery of reparative images

Let's turn to some of the images that were shared in the workshops to add some colour and form to what such energy feels like and the preciousness that we want to hold on to and make our own. Some are likely to work more than others for you – or quite different images might come to mind. Whatever it is, ask yourself what image captures something of how you feel, the way you want to be in those moments of showing up for a coached session or contact, the way of being and the lessons you want to make your own. (By the way, the session you've been asked to stand in for is starting in less than half an hour so you'd better get your skates on!)

The first image is one I introduced and is special to me: a wide open beach with a vast blue sea stretching out to the far horizon and white surf lapping toward me.

Now, I'm fortunate to live just three minutes by flipflop from a beach. I find something enormously stilling and grounding in looking at the sea, even if only for a few minutes each day. There's the natural ebb and flow, rise and fall of the tides, every day at a slightly different time. And the sea's moods constantly change: from wildly tempestuous to an unfathomable calm. Through all the ebbs and flows there is a reassuring *constancy*.

The image holds something about how I want to be in my own coaching: a dependable presence that others (and I) can rely on and that provides a sense of stability. At the same time I want to notice and attune myself to the ever-changing moods. And note the lack of judgement: a low tide is as natural and to be expected as a high tide. I don't have to tell myself off or to "buck up and just get on with it" if I'm at a low ebb. I know, though, that an enthusiasm for what lies ahead, a concentrated focus on the person in front of me and being true to myself are what will sustain me and will in turn animate others.

And here an image one of the coaches brought connects with the idea of the *enthusiasm* and excitement about the adventures we embark on. She shared an image of a hand reaching up a ladder, the top of which seemed to extend high up into an out of focus blue sky. The image conveyed a wonderful sense of reaching into the unknown – very much like the excitement and thrilled anticipation of what lies ahead of us as one of the feelings underpinning confidence. Exactly the kind of enthusiasm to bring to our coaching.

Next up, another coach had an image of *ripples* rolling out from a drop in a pool of still water. In the discussion he drew our attention to how an action we take, how we react or respond in the moment can ripple out far and wide without us having any intention or awareness of where or who that might reach. This makes me want to be really alert and conscious of the quality of care and attentiveness I bring to my coaching, whilst acknowledging that I can't control how others, around and beyond me, respond.

Another image I was keen to share is one that sits by my desk at home. It shows a small, silhouetted figure of a lone mountaineer at the top of a high, snow-capped mountain, gazing far off into the distance, the early morning sun rising and low clouds covering the valleys far below. It reminds me that in those moments of being at my very peak I feel a *stillness* and calm – not a frenetic, full-on hyper energy but something almost serene and timeless, a humbling and joyful sense of being lost and found in the wonder of the moment. How lucky am I to be here, a part of what is unfolding.

And finally, a salutary image we looked at was of a drain after a storm, the ground around it littered with washed-up debris – mud, bedraggled leaves, all strewn around the kerb-side grate. A visual representation of how we can feel that everything around us is rubbish, a mess and somehow hopeless when we are drained and wrung out. Later on we might look back and realize that even in the bleakest moments, not everything was rubbish – but at the time what a disabling, undermining feeling bears down on us. Hard to see our way through the mess. Being told to look for the positives doesn't quite do it.

What images come to your mind? What is it about them that help show something of how you feel right now? And are there images that capture how you want to be at your best, the qualities you value, what you want to hold on to and make your own?

Now, if we can know in ourselves how each quality of energy feels and can see and feed off what it enables in others, then the ways of seeking it out, nurturing and protecting it have a way of becoming obvious. For example, to be able to give that attentive, concentrated focus on the person in front of me, I have to unclutter all the noise in my head, to find a sense of perspective, ground myself in what really counts for me and put the past in its place so I can focus on the very moment ahead of me. There lies the wonder-filled, stilling calmness. And to summon up that sense of wholeheartedness might require me to consciously stop judging and comparing myself to how I imagine others think of me. To let go of perfectionism. To remind myself of what I truly value – revisit my Life Stone from Chapter 3. I want to nurture a sense of belonging to and being at ease with myself. And with that the day-to-day decisions of looking after my health and wellbeing seem to naturally follow without much thought.

In this respect, this chapter could have been a list of common sense practices that would apply to anyone. No doubt the very things we would encourage those we coach to follow. The thing about "common sense", though, is that too often it is not so common – otherwise why would we need to remind ourselves of it? More importantly, we are far more likely to act on and sustain such practices and habits when they come from a place of identifying the qualities of energy that we want to bring, captured and enriched by imagining what that might look and feel like.

The look and feel of care and support

In the Preface I highlighted the value of the various peer support groups I belong to and mentoring – both as a mentor and the one being mentored. I suggested that when we are able to share openly our feelings, reflections and experiences, rather than jumping to fix-it solutions, there is an element of being pioneers – exploring and discovering together in a supportive, respectful way. And just as we want to create spaces for those we coach to learn and find the best of themselves, so there can be a powerful, restorative effect in creating a space in which we are comfortable to look at what we feel, to express it without fear of judgement.

Before jumping to the conclusion that every coach should have some form of supportive network and mentor, true though that undoubtedly is, it is perhaps worth pausing to ask ourselves two quite challenging questions. First, what would support look and feel like? What will help us most? We might ask ourselves: what are we really after from those around us – and why? Where does the sense of need, whatever form that might take, come from? What is it hooking in to?

I suspect when we can do that, two things will naturally happen. First, we come to be more at ease with ourselves, more attuned to our inner resources and less concerned about whether those around us are providing what we had thought we needed or wanted. And second, I suspect we also become more open and able to value more deeply the richness of connections we have with friends, family, colleagues, brief one-off chance encounters and longer-term relationships, people inside and outside of our sports – seeing the uniqueness of each for what they are.

Remember our theme of the skilful art of open responses (as opposed to closed reactions) that we saw in Chapter 3: Confident coaches? And how every meaningful relationship starts with a connection, as we saw in Chapter 4: Confidence in the coach – being present, mastering the moment and holding in mind the best intent and shared purpose? These are skills at the heart of the way we want to coach and they run through every contact we make.

A call for caring cultures

The second challenging question goes to an uncomfortable, if obvious, truth. The places in which we typically coach are too often not noted for their kindness. There is a risk in concentrating on how we as coaches protect our energy that the focus ends up all on our self-care, how we look after ourselves – without properly recognizing what it is that so much effort needs to be expended to protect ourselves from.

Imagine for a moment what sports organizations – your national sports body, the professional club that employs you or the local club where you volunteer – would be like if there was a genuine culture of caring. How would that look and feel? And how different to what you know and experience now?

In the business world the culture of an organization is sometimes talked about as "the way we do things round here". I see this as having several layers. There's something about how people treat each other within and outside the organization, the style and tone of interactions – what's implicitly taken as the norm. At the same time what gets valued, rewarded, given space and resource, prioritized and singled out as great skills or achievements all come to symbolize, help shape and express the culture. Sometimes, though not always as consistently aligned and thoroughgoing as needed, these are also reflected and reinforced at the level of systems, rules and routines put in place to keep the organization functioning.

Now, I believe that the ideas and practices described in this book, which place confidence at the centre of all we do, would have a deeply transformative, freeing effect on the culture of many sports organizations: the way we interact, the things we value and the systems in place. But what a radical, hard to undertake change this would be for many.

Imagine a coaching environment – wherever it may be and at whatever level – in which, as we have suggested, everything starts from the uniqueness of the person in front of us; in which their aspirations and hopes are treated with the utmost respect as a precious gift we are privileged to share. One in which we are encouraged to know and be true to ourselves and our values. Inevitably such openness and regard would feed into every relationship and contact with others – coaching colleagues, staff, parents.

Imagine, too, that our most highly valued skills and expertise belonged in the realm of feelings and what is meaningful to each of us, coach and coached; of understanding emotions and being attuned to sensations in the body, all before the words. Wouldn't that bring a self-awareness and calming sensitivity to all we encounter along the way? What if our assessments for those qualifying at different levels of coaching, annual coaching awards or criteria for progression were about the calm, compassionate, curious attentiveness Stephen Rollnick talks of and we suggested as our highest skills?

And how about reorientating and reengineering our organizations and the supportive systems in such a way that their primary, overriding purpose was to promote creative, constant learning and deeply respectful, caring environments?

Is it fanciful? Maybe, but ask yourself: is the environment and the culture you are currently a part of as supportive, caring and dedicated to beyond belief accomplishments as it could be? And truth be told, culture is not something "out there" that comes to us fully formed and unchangeable, that we must passively accept as a given. We all have a part in creating the differences we want to see, the people we want to be – or in following along and, in so doing, replicating and reinforcing the established "normal".

All of which brings us neatly to our final Reflective Conversation – this one with the co-founder of MI, friend and mentor Professor Stephen Rollnick.

Reflective Conversation: On kindness with Professor Stephen Rollnick

Over the last two years of research and writing this book I have had many conversations with Steve as he generously reviewed and commented on each draft chapter. In our most recent conversation, now at the end of writing the book, I was keen to get Steve's view of what he sees in the many clubs and sporting organizations he visits.

I was thinking of the M.C. Escher image of a transition from one way of being to another: the hard to discern shape of our high-flying birds, their form somehow disconnected and unclear. Does he see the old, taken for granted ways of coaching – of the coach as expert to compliant athletes – beginning to shift? Or to use another metaphor we have drawn on throughout the book, what's the current landscape of coaching looking like to him? For all the talk of athlete-centred coaching, what does he see in professional team sports environments?

Shadows and light

Steve was quick to disarmingly say he is something of a grasshopper, jumping from one organization or club and on to the next – so not immersing himself in deep dives into each set-up. Yet how quickly, he said, it is possible to get a feel for the culture and the environment – the warmth of a welcome, the interest shown in everyone who enters, the easiness and respect between all who work there. Or, in contrast, the superficiality of contacts, the edginess of those engrossed in their busy tasks, that the overriding sense of "what we are here for" is first and foremost the wins, ranking positions, performance.

And something that Steve sees in those organizations and clubs where there seems to be a lightness, a joy and celebration of "good people with good ideas", as he described it, is that the deeper personal development of the coach comes first, then how they work with the athletes. But how often Steve finds himself shocked by what he called the "shadow side" of coaching – a deep-seated inertia, if not outright resistance to change and the more human approach we both aspire to.

The impression I had from his many contacts in professional team sports was of some beams of light in an otherwise shadowy, slow to change world. Within some environments he sees exciting change underway, great practice being explored and developed. Yet so much of what persists out there is the conventional, autocratic style of coaching – the coach as the deliverer of expert instruction to more or less compliant athletes. Also evident is a toxic effect of relentlessly focusing on results, on performance, medals and wins above all else. And so much of what passes for coach education reinforces these assumed ways of being – classroom edicts and the filling of heads with what-to-do prescriptions.

During our conversation Steve recounted two very different examples of the shadow and light of coaching, both in professional, high profile settings. In one, a bowler is practising in the nets under the watchful eye of an impassive coach. After one slightly off-centre delivery the coach says "That was wide", turns their back to the bowler and walks away. A small, seemingly trivial incident – yet as Steve recounted, for the bowler yet another instance in a constantly wearing, undermining pattern of belittling behaviour. The coach as better-than, quick to pass judgement and uninterested in the impact on the player beyond pointing out the blindingly obvious.

And what a contrast with another example, where Steve was about to be introduced to around 90 coaching staff at a top Premier League football academy. The Head Coach said he first needed to inform everyone that one of their young academy members had very recently suffered a bereavement and so for everyone to be mindful of what the young player must be going through, to give them space and attentive care. As he spoke, tears rolled down the coach's face. No one amongst the staff seemed to see this as a cause for embarrassment, nor did the coach appear to feel the need to apologize for their display of heartfelt emotion.

What does this small incident reflect? Steve's sense from his short time in the academy and in some other settings he visits is of a palpable, genuine kindness that runs through everything. A dedication to developing young people guiding and informing each and every development plan, the support not just from coaches but also from specialists and other staff, the design of each coaching session, the tone of conversations… and so much more.

And seeing such compassionate, caring environments makes it all the more upsetting when we are confronted with the still all too prevalent shadow side of coaching. Yet the academy and many other examples he recounts in our numerous conversations tell us that it doesn't have to be the conventional way, that doing things differently is possible even in the highest, most pressured settings. Interestingly, in our conversations, we also tell each other of acts of sublime coaching sensitivity and insight in the simplest, grassroots locations, out of the limelight through Steve's Three Cs: a calm, compassionate, curious attentiveness to the nervous, unsure of themselves person in front of the coach.

Transferability

One other question I wanted to explore with Steve in our recent conversation came out of an MI workshop I attended a few months earlier. MI was originally founded in healthcare work with people struggling with addictions. Yet at the workshop I was struck by the extraordinary spread of areas that the 100 or so participants worked in. A range of specialists working in support for various addictions for sure, including gambling and social media as well as substance abuses. Also dieticians (by the coachload as it happened). Social workers and others involved in family support. Sports coaches from many different sports and at different levels. And more. I wanted to ask Steve what enables such a diverse mix of areas to find value in MI skills.

Steve emphasized the relevance to any and all who support others to change and grow. The basic MI premise is obviously applicable to so many areas: that people are far more likely to find a way through self-limiting or harmful behaviours to healthier, more fulfilling lives if they are listened to without judgement and guided to connect with the part of themselves that, however hesitantly, wants to change. The crossovers to sports coaching are obvious, both deploying skilful listening and evoking change.

And I see a relevance running through so many of the stories recounted in this book of our resolute warriors, facing extraordinary challenges and somehow finding a way through. Their struggles with uncertainty, feeling out of place and beyond what they can do. The coach not as a provider of ready-made fix-its and formulaic solutions but ready to listen, to understand and then creatively explore together new possibilities. And in this way we can help those we coach find the excitement, stilling composure and in the moment fluency that underlie what we take to be confidence, with extraordinary results following.

Another reason for the wide transferability – and one Steve didn't mention but I know stands out for many of us who have come across MI – is his and his co-founders' openness and generosity. There is no trademarked ring-fencing or restricted access to the knowledge embodied in MI. I see a generosity of spirit, sometimes even a bemused surprise about the wide application. Steve excitedly told me about a recent paper he had been sent by a family lawyer, demonstrating how MI's approach of empathic listening could be applied in the highly confrontational, adversarial settings of family breakups going through court. The same inquisitive openness is to be enjoyed in regular (free of charge) webinars that Steve and his colleagues hold on a very wide range of related subjects, drawing in audiences of hundreds across the globe and guests ready to openly share their ideas and experiences.

Now think of your typical coach, protective of their hard-earned knowledge, as if they are somehow diminished by sharing too much. We talk about the "secrets" of a coach's methods or their success. On some coaching forums you can even come across intense debates about non-disclosure agreements prospective clients are required to sign. Of course the irony – as we saw in Chapter 4: Confidence in the coach – is that relationships of trust, of an easy mutual respect and generosity, implicitly understood and taken as the norm without the need for legalistic contracts, are where the coaching comes alive and coach and coached surprise themselves with what they can do.

Essence

In terms of how ideas are shared, spread and take hold in so many diverse areas, Steve highlighted the importance of being able to capture and communicate the essence, as he termed it, of seemingly complex ideas. In this way, others will see the relevance and apply the same ideas to their very different fields of work. I recalled that in the MI workshop, when participants were grappling with the detail of what to do, how to deal with the intricacies or challenging demands of their situation, Steve would bring us back to the essence – what are we trying to do here? Where do we want to get to? Remember the Reflective Conversation with Choreographer Anne Colvin – how she brought her dancers back to the underlying purpose whenever they appeared to become lost or overwhelmed by the technicalities of what to do? What a powerful lesson for us in our coaching.

And I wonder about the transferability of the ideas and practices explored in this book. "What's the essence?" I hear Steve ask. I go back to the very opening pages – at its heart this book is about helping us find an *easy fluency*, a being *wholly attuned* body and mind to self and others, and a depth of *meaning-filled connections*. For coach and coached alike. And for others? Imagine how powerful, enriching and enjoyable it would be to carry such an essence into our everyday relationships as well as into any range of specialist professions and practices, workplaces and communities. Something to explore in the future, perhaps.

But there we must leave our last Reflective Conversation of this book. Before we come to some final, concluding thoughts, I take with me the following:

- the idea that it is our energy – as in our enthusiasm and thrilled anticipation for whatever may lie ahead; our skilled, attentive concentration; and resolute commitment to being true to ourselves and our values – that is our most precious asset to tend to, protect and nurture

- that much like ripples through still water, we can never know how far what we do, how we treat others, how we leave them feeling will reach and impact on their lives and in turn those around them – so better to make it nurturing rather than ego-driven and self-serving

- the richness we can find for our coaching and in our lives when we can be open to the extraordinary, endless diversity of those around us, learning all the time and touched by each individual story and encounter

- finally, what greater calling can there be than to bring kindness to the places where we coach, to those we are privileged to coach and to ourselves?

Final words: On hope

THIS BOOK HAS covered a lot of ground – and all by starting from a curious paradox: that what we think and talk of as confidence may actually be an enigma; that we feel its absence but not its presence. What we do feel and can seek out and nurture are feelings of excitement as a thrilled anticipation of what might lie ahead; of a stilling, composed readiness and control, alongside an easiness with those things we can't control; and a magical, in the moment fluency in which we lose and find ourselves at our most alive. And these apply both to us in our coaching and to those we coach.

From this vantage point, of looking at confidence and the richness and depth of what is felt before the words, a whole new landscape opens up before us. One in which:

- our own self-confidence is rooted in being true to ourselves; letting go of the assumption that we have to have ready-made, expert answers to everything; trusting our intuitive "knowing in action"

- the athlete's trust and confidence in us lie not so much in an assumed role or even in the breadth and depth of our expertise (valuable though that is), but in the quality of connections; an easy mutual respect; and a sense of exploring together what is possible

- we support and guide those we coach to face their daunting challenges, surprising themselves with what they can do and creating in the moment living masterpieces of fluency and beyond belief, rich in meaning experiences.

So above all this is a book of hope – of finding better, more impactful and rewarding ways of coaching; of being at ease, losing and finding ourselves in the fluency of coaching in assured spaces we create for ourselves and others; and helping those we coach go far beyond what they believed to be possible.

We opened the book also suggesting that there is an element of courage that is needed – to rethink deeply ingrained assumptions about coaching in general and confidence in particular. In this respect, perhaps the most challenging elements involve a letting go of the limiting preconceptions we put on ourselves or allow others to impose. Coaching really doesn't have to be the conventional way it is typically thought of – nor how we are typically taught to coach.

Just imagine how different each encounter we have, each contact and connection with those we coach might be if we grounded ourselves in the approach outlined in this book:

- that everything starts from the uniqueness of the person in front of us

- treating their ambitions with the utmost respect, as a precious gift we are privileged to share

- stilling ourselves to know what we truly value and to be completely attuned to those we are with and to ourselves

- in turn, helping those we coach to be attuned to what is going on for them, nurturing a relaxed alertness to form, effort and fluency

- practising the skilful art of open responses, listening with a calm, compassionate, curious attentiveness

- finding and losing ourselves in the creative artistry of all that we do

- having a clear sense of our values and how we can make a difference.

These are just some of the distinctive, standout features, contours and colours of a wholly different landscape we can make our own.

"Hope locates itself in the premises that we don't know what will happen and that in the spaciousness of uncertainty is room to act."

Rebecca Solnit[51]

---

[51] From R. Solnit *Hope in the Dark: Untold histories, wild possibilities* (2016).

One final thought. A constant theme in the book has also been uncertainty – accepting we don't have all the answers and, in truth, don't know what will happen: whether hoped for results we and those we coach have worked so hard for will, in the end, materialize; whether all our heartfelt commitment to others will be returned; whether being ourselves will be enough. So there's an element of faith in ourselves and others. Of believing, as a fundamental principle, in the amazing things we and those we coach can do. And it is precisely in this *spaciousness of uncertainty* – as Rebecca Solnit calls it – that we have the chance to find the extraordinary beauty and power of making a difference in our coaching.

How lucky we are!

With thanks

WHERE TO START when you come to the end of a book and look back on how you got there? It's not like there is one single, direct line but a mix of zigzagging, interweaving paths with many people leaving imprints of kindness and generosity.

My journey to becoming a coach started with being coached by Roy Taylor who modelled a generous, attentive interest. Many years later, Nick Finch was there at the right time to start ZigZag Cycling with me, sharing our excitement and rawness in becoming mountain bike leaders and tutors. When it didn't work out as a business, Matt Honey encouraged me on a path to becoming a triathlon coach. Chris Roberts, Simon Ward and Rob Griffith were amongst many inspiring, generous tutors. Paula George supported me as a calm and attentive mentor. Paul Newsome and Adam Young at Swim Smooth laid a solid foundation for my swim coaching.

I have had the immense privilege of coaching many people at what became ZigZag Alive: some long term through a succession of exciting, deeply rewarding challenges; others in enriching one-off sessions. I also learnt so much in several warm hearted clubs, notably Horsham Amphibians, Brighton Tri Club and TriStars. Young Level Water swimmers continue to bring an exuberant joy and Mental Health Swims a calming stillness – special thanks to Ian Thwaites and Rachel Ashe. Through all these I learnt the true meaning and magic of confidence and self-belief.

Cindy Cox took my tentative ideas and helped give shape and energy to Confidence-Centred Coaching as something real and solid to share with other coaches.

Some journeys run their course, other take unexpected turns, yet in their time are so precious and nourishing. I am enormously grateful to Professor Howie Rush for creating a space for me in academia that served as a much needed refuge. Kate Rew provided Swim Coach Residency in the Outdoor Swimming Society. The Kearneys created a wonderful home for me to develop my Sensational Swimming. Big thanks to all.

Another journey is writing the book itself. This started with friend and mentor Steve Rollnick saying "you've got to get this stuff down in a book." He reviewed each chapter and shared stories over more than two years of research and writing. Psychotherapist Alice Hartmann provided tender, insightful support all the way through and much more beyond the writing. Cath Bishop gave enthusiastic encouragement, sharing ideas and contacts. The late Jurg Gotz, Elizabeth Egan, Martin Dighton, Rusty Earnshaw, Claire Pedrick are among others who believed and helped open doors.

Many thanks too to all those who so openly shared their experiences and thoughts, some captured in the Reflective Conversations, others in forums, workshops and peer support groups. Their stories and insights ripple through and enrich the book.

On to the publishing and Alison Jones – the "ninja" (as Claire described her to me) at Practical Inspiration Publishing – who's commitment to a better way of publishing, incisive guidance and wholehearted energy made this part of the journey feel like I'd found a home. Many thanks to her, Michelle, Shell, Frances and Nim, and the extended team of Enya Holland, Lizzie Evans, Karl Hunt and Chris Stanners.

Thanks too to the M.C. Escher Foundation, The School of Life, Anja Lechner, Michael Gervais and Meg Jay for gracious permission to use their print and words. And to Matt Walker of Cave and Sky for the illustrations.

The deepest and maybe hardest journey has been a personal one, through twists and turns of starting anew. I am so grateful to lovely and loving Annie B for patiently being there at the start and all the way through. Many more adventures to come.

About the author

MIKE PORTEOUS SET up and runs an endurance sports coaching business, ZigZag Alive, and is the founder of confidence-centred coaching: a resource for coaches across all sports that captures, shares and extends great coaching practice centred on confidence and self-belief. A highly qualified coach who represented his country as a triathlete, he now mentors British Triathlon coaches. His long and varied career has zigzagged between academia (a DPhil that took him to Brazil), government (leading high profile change programmes) and now coaching and coach development. He has been Head Coach at Brighton Tri Club (Triathlon England Club of the Year 2015) and Swim Coach in Residence at the Outdoor Swimming Society. And he teaches disabled children to swim through the charity Level Water, is a co-host and host mentor for Mental Health Swims and an advocate Butterfly for the True Athlete Project. He lives three minutes by flipflop from a beach and swims and dips through the year.

For more on confidence-centred coaching, blogs, workshops and more, check out www.zigzagconfidence.com

Index

A quick word from Practical Inspiration Publishing...

We hope you found this book both practical and inspiring – that's what we aim for with every book we publish.

We publish titles on topics ranging from leadership, entrepreneurship, HR and marketing to self-development and wellbeing.

Find details of all our books at: www.practicalinspiration.com

 **Did you know...**

We can offer discounts on bulk sales of all our titles – ideal if you want to use them for training purposes, corporate giveaways or simply because you feel these ideas deserve to be shared with your network.

We can even produce bespoke versions of our books, for example with your organization's logo and/or a tailored foreword.

To discuss further, contact us on info@practicalinspiration.com.

 **Got an idea for a business book?**

We may be able to help. Find out more about publishing in partnership with us at: bit.ly/PIpublishing.

Follow us on social media...

 @PIPTalking

 @pip_talking

 @practicalinspiration

 @piptalking

 Practical Inspiration Publishing